SECRETS OF A NUN

SECRETS OF A NUN
My Own Story

ELIZABETH UPTON

William Morrow and Company, Inc., New York

My book is based on my life as a nun. Some experiences have been consolidated in symbolic expression and some people have been presented as composite characters, with names and locations changed to protect their privacy.

Library of Congress Cataloging in Publication Data

Upton, Elizabeth.
Secrets of a nun.

1. Upton, Elizabeth.   2. Ex-nuns—United States—
Biography.   I. Title.
BX4668.3.U67A37   1985   271'.97 [B]   84-14828
ISBN: 0-688-04187-6

Printed in the United States of America

2 3 4 5 6 7 8 9 10

BOOK DESIGN BY ABBY KAGAN

To my mother and my twin, Eileen

ACKNOWLEDGMENTS

Writing this book has been a remarkable passage of insight and determination. Many—through their talents and encouragement—have assisted me along the way, for which I am grateful. But there **have** been those special few who never left my side in my brightest and darkest moments, especially Eileen, my twin, Melvin, who supported me throughout this project, and Ramtha, who gave me hope.

Particular thanks to my very gifted editor, Kay Lincks, of Marina del Rey, and to our friend Jim Bush for getting us together; to Paula Diamond, the best agent anyone could hope for; to my niece Cynthia and her husband Mike Scarpace; to the Rev. Kathleen Michele, Anna Gold, my typist, Lorna De Pute, and Michael Hamilburg, and to Jim Landis and Jane Meara of William Morrow.

And to you, the reader, for whom this book has been written.

ST. JOSEPH'S CONVENT
New York, New York

❦ 1 ❦

All the days of my life.

I knelt in front of the priest. "Reverend Mother," he addressed our directoress. "Do you accept Sister Roseann as a member of your Congregation for the rest of her religious life?"

The long, graceful fingers of her folded hands barely touched. "We do, and, with God's grace, she will remain *faithful* all the days of her life." Bowing toward the tabernacle, she moved to her kneeler at the left of the altar.

Every muscle in my body sprang free, alive, and unbound with spiritual energy. It was Jesus I would live for, would love more than husband, more than parent. The priest's voice sounded strangely calm through my excitement.

"Pronounce then, Sister Roseann, your final vows."

I pulled a breath deep into my lungs and held it, then released its flow slowly, trying to control the shaking in my voice. "I, Elizabeth Upton, called in religion Sister Roseann, do solemnly take my vows of poverty, chastity, and obedience in this Congregation of Social Work Sisters of Immaculate Mary and, with God's grace, I will persevere."

All the days of my life.

* * *

Just two weeks before, Mother Edmond had glided down the carved oak staircase of the Motherhouse, as studiedly beautiful as on the day I had met her six years before. We were not strangers to each other's distinctly different ways, and I stood up to greet her with respect. She grasped my hand and shook it enthusiastically. Six years earlier we had hugged each other warmly. It was the custom then, before Mother Edmond replaced the old Mother Foundress as our first Mother General.

"You'll be joining a fervent and loving community of Sisters. They will be your new family," Mother Edmond had written before she ascended to Mother Generalship of the Order.

I sighed deeply as Mother Edmond fastened her gaze on me.

"You still don't approve of my ban on hugging and kissing between Sisters, do you, Sister Roseann? Sit down please, please." She gestured gracefully, not allowing my reply.

Her expressive eyebrows lifted slightly. "As you know, Sister Roseann, canon law requires that the Congregation be certain," her controlled voice edged higher, "that you have the right disposition to take your final vows." She folded her thin fingers into a steeple of reflection. "My dear Sister, this is a decision of the gravest nature."

I knew this last formal interrogation offered me the chance to change my mind before I took final vows. Somehow, I felt this was the true ceremony and the ritual to come would be the celebration, not the commitment.

"Do you have any doubts about your religious calling?" Mother Edmond asked quietly.

"Doubts, Reverend Mother? Don't you mean temptations?"

She stirred in her straight chair. "Questioning? Still you question, Roseann. And that you suggest I meant temptations, when I distinctly said doubts, tells me that you may not be ready," she added firmly. Then her lips parted in what had always passed as a smile for her. "Doubts can be temptations and temptations can be doubts, especially in the year before final vows."

"From the deepest part of me, Mother, I do feel unworthy to be the Bride of Christ." I wanted to bare my child's soul and confide my fears to this woman, the real fears that had brought me to the convent in the first place. Yet, like a child, I also feared to be judged. She lifted her chin and looked out the window at the garden shrine of Jesus crucified. Anxiously, I watched her.

"And who is worthy?" she asked sadly. Now brusque, she continued, "Superficial interrogation is not my method, Sister Roseann. I prefer silence. It will allow you to examine your real motivation and examine your reason for interrupting when I speak rather than hearing what I say. It indicates that you may not be prepared for this examination."

Sweat began to dampen my black wool habit. Reflect? I knew my motivations were tainted. Wasn't it enough to leave my family, to save souls for Jesus? But when I had made that choice, I was selfish and consumed by spiritual security which I did not now feel. If I became a nun, I would certainly go straight to heaven. Or would I? It was the blistering sore of this question that had never really healed and I could feel its rawness now.

From the time I started school I had longed to emulate my nun teachers; I saw myself as mysteriously holy, encased in black and white flowing garments, saving the pagan Africans whose pictures I had avidly devoured in the pages of *National Geographic* magazine. I had vowed I would teach and feed these bony, starved, and godless poor. I went to church daily in those summers to watch Uncle Henry, a Marian priest, say Mass in our parish church, a magnificent Spanish gothic edifice. It brought me joy and peace.

Mother Edmond stirred slightly in her chair, allowing herself the least amount of comfort her rigid rule of discipline would permit her, and as if reading my mind, she said, "Personal motivation is complex, but never question the reasons why you chose to become a nun. They served the purpose of bringing you to us, to bring you to the religious life, Sister Roseann."

I looked at her carefully for a moment without the customary gesture of lowering my eyes. Yes, she represented "the religious life" to me. Her skin was pale and smooth yet somehow seemed to glow, leaving her looking much younger than her nearly fifty years. She was slender and always erect, but she moved with a graceful repose, seeming to be much taller than she really was.

I continued to look steadily at her. "I desire to take my vows for life. If this were an easy accomplishment, I think my commitment to Christ would be sorely lacking."

Mother Edmond's expression softened. "You were only fifteen when you entered our Congregation. And how old are you now?"

"Twenty-one."

She rose slowly from her chair. "Come with me," she said easily, holding out her hand.

I took it, grasping only the tips of her fingers, afraid to take more. We passed before the cobblestone chapel and bowed our heads. I could paint every inch of this hallowed sanctuary in my sleep. As a novice, I had polished brass candlesticks, stripped, waxed, and buffed the floors, and ironed stiff, starched linen. Still concerned that our conference wasn't over, I wondered if she still had more questions or if she had already deemed me unworthy. Silently, we walked into the garden toward the Stations of the Cross encircling a small cemetery. I filled my lungs with the scent of pine from the nearby woods.

"Let us talk again in an hour's time. Pray and reflect about our discussion," she said, not turning, then continued on alone.

I genuflected at the first Station of the Cross: "I adore thee, O Christ, and bless thee." At the second station, I knotted my habit skirt tightly and twisted it around my belt as I looked to the pine trees, bottle bush, and pussy willows.

Poverty, chastity, and obedience for the rest of my days? Forever a nun? I had lived my vows thus far.

Bending over, I retied my shoe laces tight, near to breaking. Then, pushing forward urgently, legs lifting high, I began to run. I sucked in hot air, my lungs expanding as the breeze bathed my face, swinging my arms in rhythm with my legs. In total abandon, I swooped off my veil. As I ran, I felt the weight of my stiff, heavy black shoes cramping my stride. It hadn't always been this way, at least not when I first knew that I could run fast. "Let me run through you and with you, Roseann; you are My Body, the Body of Christ. Sainthood is the eternal reward; you have nothing to fear." Straining, the muscles cramped in my sadly unused twenty-one-year-old body. Only six years ago my twin sister, Eileen, and I had made the 1950 Junior Olympic track team, but now I was fighting for air until I dropped, exhausted, on a soft bed of pine needles.

Our coach, Jack Smith, was head coach for the Los Angeles Olympic track team. He would look at his stopwatch and shout, "Faster! Come on, move, move, move!"

Eileen and I snorted like race horses, keeping pace step for step, identical legs pumping, identical hearts pounding, carbon-copy mouths sucking air. Eileen began to press ahead, just a hair, then a pace. Dammit! I pushed harder, stretching long, muscular fifteen-year-old legs until the muscles cramped. The white line disappeared under my feet. Oh damn, damn; Eileen beat me. Again. No matter that she cleared the line just barely ahead of me; the fact was that she always did.

Jack smiled in deep satisfaction, his sandy hair lifted into spikes by the breeze. "Okay, kids. That's it. You're both ready for the Junior Olympics." We screamed in unison.

If I hadn't had the sports, my freshman year would have been unbearable. Everything about high school was depressing, with boring subjects and girls, girls, girls. Not having boys around took the spice out of school. Being a twin was handy. Whenever I didn't feel like going to school, Eileen covered for me. The nuns couldn't tell us apart and seeing one was like seeing two. I enjoyed my hooky vacations, playing tennis, visiting museums, sometimes lying around in bed and hoping our mother would not appear early from work to catch me before I finished another library book.

Seven different orders of nuns taught at Catholic High in Los Angeles, nuns with their heads encased in white starched linen and bodies swathed in long black, brown, even blue habits. I often wondered what they thought about and whether they had the same feelings as ordinary people. They were awesome, projecting an aura that I admired but feared a little, too. So I watched and wondered. It helped the big wall clocks move around to three o'clock a little faster. And then we were free to run and run and run.

When my twin and I weren't running track in the late afternoon, we liked walking down Pico Street, titillating ourselves with being near wickedness, the endless evil-smelling beer joints and drunks and ladies of the day and night. We took turns picking which bars we would peek into. Carefully, we would part gaudy curtains screening open doorways. Country music sounded from juke boxes. We stared at couples swaying and bouncing to the music, peered, curiously to see large male arms moving unceasingly around the waists of the women or sliding down to rub satin-clad bottoms. We would gawk, always amazed, until the barkeeper yelled us out, and then we would run a little, as if terrified by his voice. But the barkeepers had learned to expect us and the peeking, and the yelling and the running was our game.

So once, when I heard my favorite song blaring through the curtains of Duffy's Bar, I pulled Eileen with me close to the doorway and hung around, bobbing my body to the beat. Suddenly angry voices rose above the music and a woman screamed in rage, "I'm gonna kill you, you motherfucker. I gonna pure kill your ass!"

"Who you talkin' to? You jus' shove it, broad. Don' give

me no crap. You nothin' but a . . ." A dark-haired man staggered through the flimsy fabric at the doorway, almost pulling it down on his big shoulders. "You nothin' but a . . ." The woman running out after him held an open switchblade in her hand, but uncertainly, as if she'd forgotten it was there. The man found his word: "You a low-down filthy hoor." He punctuated his contempt with a deep hawking and a gob of spit dumped on the woman's sandal. She gave a wild shriek of fury and suddenly slashed at the man, who swayed drunkenly before her and pulled his arm up to fend off the knife as a ghastly slit crossed his face, puncturing his eye and opening his nose so that blood jetted in terrible spurts. A huge bouncer plunged through the doorway and grabbed the woman, but she nicked his arm before he hit her jaw with his enormous fist and she dropped to the pavement.

Pico Street no longer seemed a playful, friendly, and familiar naughtiness, but a world of danger and obscene pain that could so easily sweep me into its awfulness. Well, at least I wouldn't go to Pico Street for a long time, not until I prayed for those people and for myself and could feel I walked protected by the gentle power of the Madonna. But the prayers didn't wipe out my memory of the furious woman's face and the bloody man's face and, finally, the limp, unconscious body of the battered woman. What would they do, the man with one blind eye and the woman locked away? Somehow, my distress over their shocking futures gradually obliterated my terror and I seemed to be thinking more often about little stories of how I would plead successfully to the judge for the woman's freedom or become a famous woman doctor who was able to restore the man's sight. Or maybe I would dedicate my life to treading Pico Street fearlessly, bringing hope and the comfort of God to the homeless, inspiring the wicked ones to change and become good, kind people. . . . I think that may have been the first step starting me on the journey that brought me to this pinewoods, to the commitment to serve God as a social work nun.

The drive to help deepened in me until it was a passion I lived with every day. School work, never too attractive, lost all appeal. The playfulness of walking Pico Street had evaporated in a single afternoon. Even running had become nothing more than a way to immerse myself temporarily in a comfortable forgetfulness. As soon as I stopped running and returned home or to classes, the pain and exasperation surged back into my consciousness.

I began to stop every day at the little jewellike chapel in downtown Los Angeles. As the months passed, I consecrated myself to the Virgin Mary, putting my heart, mind, and soul under her loving protection. She would pull me through; she would be my model for sainthood. I loved saying the Rosary, feeling the silken beads slip through my fingers, counting the Aves; and the more visits I made to the little chapel, the more exalted I felt. Mary understood me. The Mother of God was powerful and I was in need of her help.

I wrote to dozens of religious orders. If Marie and Joan, my close friends, could decide that becoming nuns was what they wanted to do with their lives, why not me? There had to be nuns who specialized in helping people with problems, and I was beginning to know that I wanted to be one of them. This was becoming my consuming preoccupation. My interest in the track team dwindled. Eileen thought I was a bit crazy. My hard-working mother, who had supported us since our father's death when we were infants, watched my changing interest but said nothing until I had spent several months immersed in my search.

"Elizabeth Anne," she said one Sunday. "What are you planning to do this summer?"

"I want to become a nun," I said, hoping I didn't shock her too much, but relieved to say it to her. Now it was finally out in the open. Resting back in her old rocker, she sat silent for a long while. Her silky black hair fell gently past her shoulders, swinging with the movement of the rocker. She was beautiful, but now her face seemed drawn. "Do you know anything about the rigors of becoming a nun? You'll have to leave home and your sister."

"It's what I really want to do most." I ran out of her bedroom and returned with a bundle of literature. "This is the order I like best. They do work I want to do. Just read these letters. And their magazines—they're wonderful! Just wonderful!" I had studied their religious schedule a hundred times. It was divided between prayer and working in the missionary field. It was good to know they didn't spend all their time in chapel, but even so, they were dedicated to nearly five hours a day of prayer.

Patiently, she looked at them. I wasn't sure if she was actually reading as she fingered through the pages. "New York?" she asked.

"I'd start out right in New York City. Imagine!"

"But you're only fifteen, my dear. You can finish school and then become a nun."

"But I want to go now. I don't want to finish school. It's so boring and I don't learn anything."

"If you're thinking of entering the New York social work order, we'll never see you again, you'll be so far from home." My mother's voice broke slightly, and my own throat tightened.

"Mother, it's what I really want to do." I had the determination and stubbornness of my mother and her mother. It was in my genes. I felt strong and confident, and my mother knew that temperament all too well. Standing up, she hugged me, but her eyes were sad.

Now, here I sat in pinewoods digging my knuckles deeper into my muscles to ease the soreness of running. Six years ago I would never have had to do that. I heard footsteps and I leaped up. A little way off in the distance stood Sister Coline, my former Novice Mistress. My veil felt heavy hanging from my hand, and I could feel heat rise to my cheeks. Quickly, she retreated. Carefully, I readjusted my veil and unknotted my habit skirt. Once more I massaged my sore muscles. Did I love my body too much?

Just as I reached the outer path at the first Station of the Cross, I saw Mother Edmond solemnly watching my return. For a painfully awkward moment we avoided each other's eyes. Then she said, "One hour's time has turned into three, Sister Roseann. Let us continue our conference here." She gestured to a stone bench. "And have you liked your missionary work?"

I felt a wave of honest excitement flush my face. "Oh, yes, especially my work in Harlem. After getting over the initial shock, of course."

"It's only the beginning, Sister. You'll experience more misery than that." She rubbed her fingers over the figure of the crucifix on the worn rosary beads hanging from her waist. "I've been told you are quite successful as a catechetical teacher in your mission, but remember that success can breed the temptation of intellectual pride." She paused, not smiling, and I felt the sting of correction for all my hard work. I believed that I had earned at least token praise.

"I realize that, Mother," I said, trying to hide my offended pride, "and it's been more difficult, I think, because of my lack of education. If I had finished high school, if I had some college education . . ."

"Perhaps," she offered coolly, "but you do have enough education to do our work. Tell me, Sister, are you at peace in your decision to take your final vows—fully, unconditionally at peace?"

"Sometimes, Reverend Mother, I feel great peace; other times, I question everything: the Holy Rule, my vows, everything." I had been more forthright than "good politics" demanded. She laughed.

"Then you admit to your human frailty?"

Surprised at her ease, I smiled. "Yes."

"If one is not tested on one's vocational calling, I would wonder seriously about the state of one's soul. Religious life is not meant to be easy, nor is the dying of one's ego or the disciplining of all one's emotions. It takes a lifetime of prayer and of sacrifice, for sainthood is nothing less than the death of self, of ego," she added thoughtfully.

Again I looked directly into her eyes. They were the outstanding feature of her serenely composed face, eyes large and very blue, with a fringe of long, dark lashes. In a community of nuns where everyone wore identical habits and learned quickly to imitate the same set of gestures, one became particularly sensitive to any outstanding features that would help distinguish one from another. With Mother Edmond it was her eyes and it gave me pleasure to look at them. But this time I could not hold her look, and I lowered my gaze in a sign of submission.

For the first time she seemed pleased with me. Then she took my hands and held them fleetingly. "May God's grace be with you all the days of your religious life and the fullness of His love and peace be your constant companion, especially during this solemn retreat of your final vows."

"Please pray for me," I asked softly.

She bowed graciously, then headed toward the chapel.

❦ 2 ❦

The chatter was at top volume. We had just been told that our retreat master was the renowned Jesuit poet, author, and psychologist Father Barrett. Although we had been denied all secular reading, including the journals for which Father Barrett wrote, a rule of Mother Edmond's, still we had heard of his famous retreats.

A wave of peace swept over me as I knelt in the simple chapel. Sister Coline, her dark skin contrasting dramatically with the white linen framing her face, paraded her novices into chapel, their eyes appropriately curtained. Coline knelt directly in front of me. She no longer held power over me, but as a novice she had been the spiritual hammer of Mother Edmond, relentlessly chiseling and molding the hard rock of my soul into an example of Mother Edmond's ideals of perfection. "My task is your spiritual formation and it is my special cross to bear," Coline reminded us too many times. I seldom felt sorry for her then or now. I had once feared Coline; the fear, but not my anger, had vanished when I left the novitiate.

In the hot humid morning the novices dripped in enforced misery. The Sisters rose from their pews in respectful salute as Father Barrett entered. He carried himself proudly as he sauntered to the front of his table. That walk was so familiar, he must have been an athlete, I thought. I liked his sandy-haired, big-boned looks.

He didn't sit down immediately, but paced pensively back and forth until finally he faced us squarely. "If you have any doubts about my experience, any doubts whatsoever, put all your fears to rest," he said. "I have six blood sisters, a spry mother who bosses her grown children. I've been a pastor, a teacher, a confessor of nuns for many years." His face brightened handsomely. "My good Sisters, I dare say I know a woman's heart." My skin tingled pleasantly and I felt a shortness of breath. Father Barrett was a priest, but at this moment, in the depths of my being, I felt his manliness, not his priestliness. His power frightened me. Would I be able to bare my soul to this . . . this man?

He sat down at the conference table in the chapel's sanctuary, his feet on the table and a cigar sticking out of his cassock pocket. The front pew was taken by three nun-stenographers, their fingers speeding across yellow lined notepads. "We will name this retreat the Retreat of the Smiling Faces." His lips spread in a generous smile, and a tremor of excitement warmed me, as I rested, unlike Mother Edmond, against the back of my oak pew. He continued, "I have taken stock of your overwhelming seriousness. I feel unnatural tension among you, and it is not healthy. It can breed sick minds and sick bodies." Mockingbirds squabbled noisily outside the chapel window, but inside no one stirred, not even to move a rosary bead.

"I've done my homework, Sisters. Incredible woman, your Foundress. But I am afraid, Sisters," he paused. His body seemed to lose its vitality, as if the importance of what he was going to say had already taken its toll. "But, Sisters, I'm afraid I sense some major departures from her nourishing spirit. It frightens me to look among you, to see the anticipation on your faces, knowing that such departures of spirit could eventually destroy your very growth as a religious order if you continue to ignore her ideas."

The Sisters shifted uneasily; a novice sneezed, then shrank as Coline's face stiffened angrily. What did Father Barrett know about the recent changes, about Mother Edmond's administrative policy? Did he know that Mother Foundress was rarely mentioned? He seemed to know more than he had any right to know.

Father Barrett had scheduled three weighty conferences a day for the duration of the retreat. Eight days of inner reflection, the spiritual exercises of St. Ignatius, and the constant presence of Father Barrett would bring us closer to Jesus, I was sure.

Next morning, Father Barrett opened his conference with a cannonade. "I am tired of watching you all parade in, doubled over like so many slaves bowed by the weight of slabs for a pharoah's pyramid." Slipping from his chair, he bobbled, grimacing, coughing, and pulling his cassock over his face until he fell into the front pew. Surprise and shock worked precisely the way he had planned it. The chapel exploded. The Retreat of the Smiling Faces had begun. "And, for God's sake, look up and see where you are going." He added, "We have sufficient blindness within Mother Church as it is!"

For the first time that I could remember, our retreat meals were enjoyed in smiles and good feelings. The corned beef and cabbage had never tasted so delicious; I wondered why I was so hungry. At my table, even the senior Sisters were hard put to suppress giggles. The change felt good, deep and warm.

The following afternoon, Father Barrett swept the chapel in a penetrating gaze, appraising us. "You're not going to forget," he said, "the grace of this retreat. Retreat masters will come and go, my dear Sisters, but remember John the Baptist, who cried, 'Make straight the way of the Lord,' and *he was called great* by Jesus. There is much to cleanse from our souls. To make way for the coming of Christ. Yes, Sisters, twenty, thirty years from now, sixty, if you're lucky, if we're still with each other, you'll be saying, 'I remember Barrett's retreat.'" We laughed at his arrogance.

Outside the chapel I watched him hover over a mounting anthill, absolutely absorbed with the activity. "Marvelous workmanship here; reminds one of the complexity of the Mystical Body of Christ, don't you think, Sister?" he asked a passing novice, who bowed nervously but kept on moving. He left the garden, but shortly he returned, wearing a startling red T-shirt, tight white pants, and worn-down tennis shoes. Gasping, I put my hand to my mouth; I could not help but watch his rippling muscles and his tight round buttocks outlined against the fabric. He swaggered toward the rear of the rectory path. I followed more slowly, keeping a distance between us. At the fork, he turned right. A feeling of guilt seized me. Why was I following him at all? Had Mother Edmond, who had just turned the corner from the Motherhouse, seen me watching him?

In past retreats the tension of the eight-day silence, of no recreation, of no conversations, of total introspection had worn heavily on my spirit, but this retreat sped by. Sisters lined up in droves at his purple-curtained confessional. He seemed to pay ample attention to each Sister, no matter how long it took. I'll make my general confession on the last day of retreat, I thought. It seemed the wisest spiritual action to take, or was I just putting it off?

With each passing day, the Sisters were found earlier in chapel, eager for Father Barrett's conference to begin. A rare phenomenon indeed. However, I began to see that none of his conference notes were being passed out, the silent but clear sign of Mother Edmond's disapproval. Oblivious of politics, I took my notes carefully, vowing never to destroy them.

One morning Father Barrett strode briskly into the chapel, speaking as he came: "Silence, unless it is filled with love, with appreciation for your emotions, will breed neurotic and psychotic nuns, in addition to encouraging the consumption of too much aspirin." He slipped into his chair heavily. "If you want to find out how spiritually healthy your religious Order is, ask yourselves how many die of cancer. Who are the young women leaving your novitiate? Are they assertive? Intellectually inquisitive? Are they threats to your unbending rules of rigidity?" A suffocating hush spread through the chapel. My head ached at the temples. He spoke of topics no one dared think about or mention.

Then suddenly we had just two days of retreat left. Father Barrett leaned over his table pointing a long thick finger at us, something he had not done before. I felt he spoke directly to me. "*Your emotions, your feelings, are God's gifts. They are the guts of your personhood. Treat them well and they will respond to you as cherished friends. Trust your instincts; that's what you have them for.* 'I have come that you may have life and have it to the full,' Jesus said. Life, my dear Sisters, means life to the *full*. Full of play, full of laughter, full of friendship, full of love, full of tears, and full of anger, and don't forget rest and relaxation." Then, as if pleading, Barrett added, "I have shared my heart with you. I have given you all I can with love and faith and . . ." He rested then on the back of his chair, exhaustion lining his face. Long conferences and hours in the confessional had finally taken their toll. "Only the truth will set you free," he said in a low voice. "If this retreat, this truth, is what you live by, if this is what you remember, even if only in your dreams, this retreat will have served Christ." He scanned our faces with fervid intensity. "I leave one question with you: who is there among you that will accept this truth, the fruit of this retreat?" Abruptly he rose, bowed profoundly before the tabernacle, and left the chapel.

My veil stuck to my face and I wiped my eyes. I felt the truth of his message in the hidden depths of my soul. I loved this priest, this man, this unwanted prophet, I said fervently to my heart. I love him. I will not deny this much to myself.

*   *   *

It was my turn. "Bless me, Father, for I have sinned and I want to make my general confession in preparation for my final vows," I whispered hoarsely.

"Yes, Sister."

A wave of peaceful calm eased my body, more because I was the last Sister in the confessional line than for what should have been a spiritual reason. Streams of sunlight pierced the cloth screen. I could see Father Barrett's face clearly, his lips, the curly sandy hair. He looked directly at me, ignoring the traditional custom of shading his eyes with his hand.

"Until I entered the convent, I lied, I stole money from my mother's purse, swore, had temper outbursts, and sinned against purity."

"Have you changed any?" His voice was too light for comfort, though I didn't mind that we looked at each other.

"I thought my religious life would have reformed me, made dramatic changes in me," I said.

Father Barrett laughed a bit too heartily, I thought. "Change of heart, change of soul take time, Sister, a lifetime."

"And I wish I didn't still have a temper."

"Why don't you say 'my temper'? You own it, don't you? Tell me about what troubles you the most."

The confessional grew intensely hot. "We're not supposed to give in to our feelings."

"And whose eternal truth is that, Sister?"

"Mother Edmond's, all our Superiors', our Holy Rule!"

"Have you gained nothing from this retreat?" he asked in a sad and gentle voice.

"Yes . . . I . . . I really have, Father," I answered.

He drew closer to the confessional screen and his warm breath reached my face. "Your feelings, your emotions are vital parts of your being. Deny them and you'll dry up like a frog, deprived of lily pads and moisture."

My words spewed out. "I loved your retreat, it made so

much sense, Father, but all my religious life I've been instructed in the opposite . . . It confuses me."

"I know, Sister." His voice again became gentle, and I felt my soul caressed. "Don't reject the truth. You'll discover its validity in God's good time."

"I feel that."

"Good. Try loving yourself, your emotions, your passions instead of fighting against them. Learn most of all to forgive yourself. It's the seed of true love." He brushed his large fingers through his hair as if he had all the time in the world just for me. "Anything more, Sister?"

"I hated old Father Briam. I even wished him dead."

"Many did, I'm told," Father Barrett said simply.

I hesitated. "He died of a sudden heart attack and . . . and . . ."

"Yes, Sister." He loosened the collar of his cassock and leaned back against his cushioned chair.

I continued, "I told Father Briam he was heartless, he was cheap . . . forcing the Sisters to teach children in a freezing church . . ."

"He sounds like a real son of a bitch. Isn't that the truth?"

"Why . . . why, I suppose so."

"Of course if you swore so much as a kid, you probably still do it in your mind. And it gets to the point fast, doesn't it?" A tinge of satisfaction underlined his voice. "Tell me, have you ever thought of Father Briam as a son of a bitch?"

I couldn't control my laughter. "You're right!"

"Ah ha!" Father Barrett rocked in his chair and laughed with me. I parted the curtains quickly, glancing out of the confessional to see if we were being heard. Only two Sisters sat in the chapel's rear pew. Sweat dripped down my face and I could taste its saltiness.

"You think you're a witch telling off the old war horse and him dying, seemingly on command? Come, come, Sister. It's not that simple. Did he have a heart condition?"

"A bad one, actually."

"Did he have young assistants?"

"Yes, two."

"Young priests speak their minds, you know. Certainly not as sweetly as you did. They probably sent him to perdition more than once, I dare say with hot passion." He paused. "His time was come. You blessed Father Briam and yourself because of your concern, your honesty. But you must forget it. Release the anger, the resentment."

I sighed deeply. If only Father Barrett were my regular confessor, I'd have a clear head and a less scrupulous soul.

"How old are you?" he asked.

"Twenty-two in five days."

"And will there be a grand celebration for your birthday?"

"Our custom is to celebrate only feast days." There was a long silence. I looked across the veiled curtain, trying to find Barrett's eyes. Had he fallen asleep?

"That's a pity, Sister," he said finally. "Now tell me what else troubles you."

"My arrogance. I'm told it's intellectual pride."

"Says who?"

"My Superiors."

"Well . . . well . . . we have a great sinner here," he said lightly. "Have you so easily forgotten that Jesus, at twelve, questioned his parents and debated the Scribes?"

"But he was Jesus," I insisted.

"You are no less the Body of Christ," his voice edged sharply. "You have a mind. Use it! If you don't, you'll become a mental cripple, and *most significantly*, you'll be of no use to yourself, to the Church, to the parishioners you serve, or to Christ Himself!"

"My God!" I whispered loudly.

"God, yes! I've seen your Congregation. It has more than its fair share of the mentally lame!"

I covered my face and coughed.

"Why do you hesitate, Sister? And what are you hiding from?"

"Because . . . because of the way you speak your mind. It scares me."

He laughed lightly. I gripped my beads, moved them through my fingers, then blurted out, "Father, I have sinned against purity, against my holy vow of chastity."

"What in particular?" he asked calmly.

"My thoughts, my desires," I said. My throat felt scorched. "I had thought after six years as a nun, chastity would be easier to deal with." I swiped at the sweat beading my forehead with the harsh woolen sleeve of my habit. "I fear that I enjoy the presence of men and of the teenage boys I teach. They fascinate me more than the company of women. They distract me at prayer. They are in my dreams."

"You're very seductive, Sister. Do you know that about yourself?" Father Barrett asked, his eyes now averted. "My dear Sister, teenage boys and men are attractive. They arouse tenderness, pleasure. This is a simple fact of human nature. It is also our cross of celibacy and it requires discipline, but that is not to deny that it exists."

I found myself unable to speak.

"You hesitate still?"

"You scare me," I said.

"Scared spiritless, I'd say. Too frightened of your feelings, your emotions, of your sexuality. But believe me, this is *not* sinful."

"That's not what I have been taught, Father."

"Ignorance!" he said disgustedly. "Tell me, Sister, did Jesus take unto himself a breed of dispirited hangers-on?"

"No."

"Indeed not. They were alive, passionate, lusty, beautiful as He was. Weren't they?"

"Yes," I answered numbly.

"You're a woman. Praise God for your emotions, for your female body, for your *breasts*, for your feelings, for God's sake and for your own sake, Sister."

My body was quivering with excitement. I pulled at the skirt of my habit, which clung heavily to my thighs. "Father, but I have fantasies. In them I make love; with me, it's a sinful disease."

"Sister, Sister, loving is what your nun's life is all about. Giving love, offering the fruits of your womanhood, your mind to Christ in His praise. Where is the sin?"

"I feel Christ chose me only *because* I am a sinner, to save me from myself."

"Have you ever thought that He seeks you as His friend, that He seeks a lover in you?" Father Barrett's eyes searched mine with a tenderness that sent the blood rushing to my face. I could feel his strength, his conviction. I could almost feel his arms drawing me into his chest, closer to his black cassock, and I yearned for this contact.

"Never lose hope," he said earnestly. "It's the cardinal virtue." Then his hand lifted slightly as he made the sign of the cross. "May God forgive you . . . and live His peace." He rose quickly.

"Father . . . my penance . . . please."

He smiled broadly. "Go into God's places, Sister. Smell deeply of the honeysuckle and praise Him." He was out of the booth easily and then left the chapel.

I sucked in the fresh air, my body drenched. Father Barrett had gone on ahead, his footsteps echoing as he turned the corner and was gone. Make up my own prayer and smell honeysuckle? Odd penance . . . strange wizard, this Father Barrett.

That night, every inch of mattress on my small wire-spring cot exuded sticky heat. My hands slid over my sheets in search of coolness. Even the summer breeze held still through the pinewood. A stream·of cars filed up the winding driveway, depositing their garrulous passengers at the rectory door. Husky laughter bounced like wild surf and Father Barrett's voice roared above the rest. I pulled the sheets over my head, swellings of envy kindling my anger at their clerical freedom. They were drinking and celebrating, indulging in freedoms forbidden to nuns. Priests were the elite, the "chosen." Raspy accordian swirls broke the quietness of the dorm, yet they did not disturb the three senior Sisters, who slept on peacefully. I tossed in my hard bed, raising myself and yanking off the stifling sheet. Heavy yellow muslin curtains mantled my quarters. The men's voices disturbed the hill's silence, and the aroma of pipes, cigars, and cigarettes aroused me.

Painstakingly, so as not to disturb the Sisters' sleep, I pulled my long cotton nightgown gingerly up over my kneecaps. A rush of cool air swept my legs. Unbound, I arched and stretched, reveling in the freedom. Grabbing up my gown, I began to twist it up higher, breathing in deeply the gentle breeze of honeysuckle and jasmine.

Wringing and twisting my nightgown into a tightened knot, I began passing it slowly back and forth beneath my buttocks, sliding it against their roundness, knotting it into a hard white cord. Familiar music buzzed through my head. "Jessie, I want you"—a song I knew from somewhere. And then a sandy-haired man hazed before me. The cord slid between my inner thighs, rubbing the tightness of my mound. I pulled it tighter and it rose and fell to a new rhythm, raw and savage. I felt like a cat, sensuous, clawing at its barred cage for release. Barrett's breath brushed across my face and I could smell him, touch his lips . . .

My gown tightened, rubbing deliciously through the burning lips of my wet vagina, flicking fiery sensations through my body as I rocked back and forth rhythmically. I want this . . . I want this . . . and mounting seering spasms leaped to consume me. The bed next to mine jerked as an asthmatic nun heaved violently. I froze. Pulling down my nightgown, I slipped out of bed and leaned against the window, shaking and staring at my bed. Dropping to the hard wooden floor, I tucked myself into a tight ball, sliding partway under the cot. I wanted to hide from myself, from my frustration, from my shame.

The next morning, torn with anxiety and guilt, I half ran toward the rectory. Father Barrett strode leisurely toward the chapel. "Father, would you . . . hear my confession? I hate to trouble you, but I . . ." Quietness of soul reflected clearly in his eyes. Did he have no memory of my last confession? I

deserved righteous anger. I wanted it. "Father, I'm too weak
. . . too undeserving of my final vows . . ." I couldn't finish
the sentence.

"Calm yourself, Sister. Jesus is not anger. He is love," he
said tenderly. "He is not an obscure metaphor. He is the
experience, the living model we set for our perfection." I
needed to believe this more now than ever before.

"Read the 'Canticle of Canticles' for your penance . . ."
he said. "And if only for today, love your most precious
self."

"How can I thank you?" I said, tears welling at the corners
of my eyes.

"Remember me in your prayers, and it is I who will be in
debt to you." Then he was gone, leaving me alone. Later,
leafing through the Old Testament, I found the verse. I didn't
understand it at first, and once more I read it over:

"How beautiful art thou my love, how beautiful art thou!
Thy hair is as flocks of goats, which come up from Galaad.
Thy two breasts like two young roses that are twins, which
feed among the lilies. Thou are all fair, O my love, and
there is not a spot in thee. How beautiful are thy breasts, my
sister, my spouse; thy breasts are more beautiful than wine,
and the sweet smell of thy ointments above all aromatical
spices. Thy lips, my spouse, are as dripping honey comb,
honey and milk are under thy tongue; and the smell of thy
garments, as the smell of frankincense."

Burying my face in my prayer-book, I wept quietly. Lord
bless this holy man, this most holy priest, Father Barrett, for
all the days of his life.

Father Barrett's gaze lingered over each Sister in the profession ceremony, resting on me, it seemed, longer than the
others. It wasn't my imagination. I felt the penetrating of his
soul communicating through the Church the values that
were his. The values I sought so desperately to have as my
own. Now he read aloud from the "Canticle of Canticles":
"Arise . . . make haste . . . my love . . . my dove, my beau-

tiful . . . and come. For winter is now past . . . the rain is over . . . and gone." He closed his eyes as he spoke the phrase " 'Come, my beloved, let us go forth into the fields, let us abide in the villages.' " His voice was tender, loving, yet I felt angry in the midst of the celebration, disappointed that he did not allow me into that special place I had imagined he had gone when he had closed his eyes. I tried to gain control for the purity of soul this moment demanded. Who was I to demand anything other than what was given me?

I watched the postulants receive their black novice habits, white starched veils, and new identities of Sister. One by one they seemed to melt into the sanctuary beyond. I shuffled my feet in anticipation of the moment when all eyes would be on me and my eyes would be on Christ. Four novices pronounced their first holy vows, looking joyfully solemn, donned in black veils and silver medallions, hanging on long black cords around their necks. But final vows was the most solemn consecration in this narrow road to sainthood.

I genuflected and knelt in front of Father Barrett.

"Reverend Mother," Barrett asked. "Do you accept Sister Roseann as a member of your Congregation for the rest of her religious life?"

"We do, and with God's grace she will remain faithful all the days of her life." Bowing toward the tabernacle, she retreated to her kneeler.

"Pronounce then, Sister Roseann, your final vows," Father Barrett said calmly, his hand almost touching my lips.

"I, Elizabeth Upton, called in religion Sister Roseann, do solemnly take my vows of poverty, chastity, and obedience in this Congregation of Social Work Sisters of Immaculate Mary. And with God's grace, I will persevere."

"Amen," Barrett replied triumphantly as he blessed my personal victory. Lowering a crown of white roses on my head, he announced, "Receive this crown of roses, the symbol of everlasting happiness and of your reward for all eternity." He then placed the six-inch ebony crucifix in my hands. "Receive this cross as the symbol of your dedication to Jesus Crucifixed, and by this cross you will win your eternal reward."

"Amen," I said as I kissed the smooth wooden cross and fixed it gently on my left side with my long rosary beads. I picked up my glowing candle and returned to my kneeler. I wanted the ecstasy of this moment in Jesus to last forever.

Father Barrett faced the Sisters and pronounced his final message: "'Who is She that cometh forth as the morning rising, fair as the moon, bright as the sun, terrible as an army set in array?'" His hands reached out slowly toward us, almost as if he wanted to touch us physically, then he rested them in front of his chasuble. "This verse from Scripture has traditionally been addressed to the Virgin Mary," he said, "but, Sisters I address these words to you . . . to your immortal spirit, for this is the key of your retreat. Reflect upon it."

At this moment I knew certainly that I was unworthy, that I was a sinner, in spite of Father Barrett's exhortations. But Jesus had always known my heart, and yet He had chosen me for Himself. I allowed myself to rejoice, to be swept up in the celebration.

Every stop of the organ was pulled out for the "Te Deum" hymn resounding from the chapel's stone walls as we processed, two by two, out of the chapel. But Barrett, even though he was engulfed by bubbling nuns and admiring clergy, found his way to my side, the eyes of curious admirers following him.

"You are most beautiful today, Sister Roseann," he said in a low voice, "crowned with white roses. I will miss your smiling at me from your chapel seat," he added.

I bowed, feeling awkward, but he continued in a quieter voice only I could hear. "Rid your holy self of this self-effacing habit of lowering your eyes," he said kindly. "You are the Bride of Christ. You wear His crown. You carry His cross." I had no choice but to lift my face up to his and meet his gaze.

Father Barrett covered both of my hands with his and, bowing slightly, touched his lips to my palms before he returned to his group. Laughter grew, and I imagined personal judgments were being made as I hurried away from the rectory. Father Barrett had kissed my hands publicly. Why? I hurried on, holding on to my white rose crown, seeking a place to hide, to think calmly. Then I headed toward the chapel stumbling through the act of contrition, "I am heartily sorry for having offended Thee." But was the kiss of praise, of love from a holy man, something to be ashamed of?

My head was ringing with happiness as I entered the Motherhouse's tiny kitchen. I plunged my wrists into cold tap water. This July was stifling hot, almost unbearable with the wearing of woolen habits. I could hear familiar voices drift toward me from the main foyer and I opened the door a crack. I could see the flushed face of Mother Edmond, not three feet from Father Barrett, her arms folded sternly across her chest. Father Barrett's feet were planted firmly, as if to stop the charge of a bull.

"I am the grinding sand against the oyster," he said, his eyes sparkling.

"You are dangerous," she fired back, her fingers working up and down the seam of her sleeves.

"Because I mean to break into these closed, hardened, censored, nun-shells? Because I mean to bring forth their souls to happy perfection? This is my intent, Mother Edmond. This is my mission." I strained to hear.

"And it is mine as well, Father," she replied, raising her voice, the Irish lilt more obvious now that she was angry. "Only in renunciation of all our passions and our emotions will the Sisters attain the heights of perfection, Father."

"Self-renunciation, Mother Edmond?" Father Barrett asked. "What about some honest self-esteem?"

Mother Edmond took two delicate steps backward. "The

Sisters will not be given your conference notes. You will receive a copy," she added, "for yourself."

"I object to your presumptions, to your rash judgment of my integrity," he said sharply. Mother Edmond grew silent. Then Father Barrett moved closer to her, raising his hand in a gesture of peace. "Enough of this . . . let us try to end our disagreement agreeably." Then, ever so faintly, the corners of Edmond's lips curled upward in a smile. And they both moved out to the rose garden. As I closed the door, I saw my former Novice Mistress, Sister Coline, standing off to the side. We looked at each other, and I read questions on her face. Ashamed, I rushed out, knowing Coline had been as absorbed in the conversation as I had.

I saw Sister Verdine half running down the gravel path toward me, her face radiant. "You'll be finding this news out soon enough," she said as she approached. "Mother Edmond has granted permission for you to work with me in Saint Ann's parish in Harlem!"

Instinctively, I reached for her. Verdine's face widened with pleasure. Harlem would be my summer assignment, and it was Mother Edmond who had said yes. Two gifts, one from Father Barrett, another from Mother Edmond. In my excitement over the missionary service to be done in Harlem, I momentarily forgot the question that troubled me. In their differences, who was the rightful representative of Christ, Father Barrett or Mother Edmond?

3

The three-story red-brick building, the Convent of Saint Joseph, smelled old and stuffy. I glanced around the empty community room. When I was here six years ago, there had been a radio in the corner, a camera, and piles of *The New York Times,* now replaced, at Mother Edmond's direction, with parish files. It saddened me somehow. A letter from Mother Edmond dominated the bulletin board. "Hold steadfast to the graces of your retreat," she had written. Where was Father Barrett, I wondered. Did he think of me . . . ever?

When I went to chapel for evening prayers, I counted the Sisters as they marched into chapel. Two Sisters had recently and invisibly left the Congregation, despairing of Mother Edmond's reform, it had been whispered. I remembered them: one round, fair, and pretty; the other, a thin nun with a slight limp. Lord, I prayed, grant me faithfulness to my holy vows. The comforting face of Father Barrett lingered in my mind's eye. Yesterday's glory seemed so far away.

Next morning, fog horns trumpeted up from the Hudson River as I prepared myself for Holy Mass. I needed to get a firm grip on my summer assignment. After breakfast, I waited for Sister Verdine at the parlor window. I watched her gliding walk as she moved through the crowd of women in their light summer dresses, leaving surrounding apartments for work. Saint Joseph's like many of our convents, was located in a residential neighborhood rather than being attached to a parish, since we often served more than one parish.

Although Verdine was only six years older than I, she had been the mistress of postulants, the step in training between novice and final vows, when I was at the Motherhouse. She was as tall and as slender as I, and I wondered as I watched her whether six years from now I would have learned to hold the rest of my body so still while my feet carried me forward in this gliding gate. Now Verdine raised her hand in her habitual gesture and brushed the veil back from her round, pretty face with its dark, expressive eyes. The gesture seemed almost defiant, as if the veil were in her way, a contrast to her otherwise calm and accepting demeanor.

"Let's go," Verdine called from the ornate oak doorway. "You'll love the Franciscan Fathers at St. Ann's," she added, her voice light with anticipation.

I nodded, cheered by her enthusiasm.

We swayed with the subway rush crowd of frantic-looking passengers until the train jerked to a stop. Humid heat rose from the streets; it was becoming unbearable too early in the morning. We passed rows of tenements that seemed to hang together by sheer endurance. I held my breath against the stench of open garbage cans. "Nothing changes," I hissed. "It's as if I had never walked these streets before." I held tighter to my small purse, annoyed that my first impressions of six years ago had faded.

"Some things are always shocking," Verdine said reassuringly as she checked her parish census cards. Pointing to the tottering building on the corner, she said, "We'll start here, together."

"I bet there isn't a family that's lived here over a year," I said, relying on my past recollections.

"No doubt, Roseann."

Three muddy-faced children with soggy pants followed our long, flowing black figures wide-eyed. Bending over, I patted a two-year-old's matted hair. "You're precious," I said. He began to chew on my beads. "No . . . you must not," I said, yanking them away.

"It's all right, Sister. He puts everything in his mouth," his mother called from a second-floor window. She yelled something in Spanish to her child, who looked up unhappily, rubbing his eyes.

The hallway was dark, stifling. I followed Verdine up the stairs, holding my skirts up, even avoiding contact with the banister. She knocked at an apartment door, announcing, "We are the Sisters from St. Ann's parish, visiting some of our families."

"Come in . . ." a voice called out from behind the door. We stepped into the kitchen. "But be careful!" A slender young woman stood on a chair, sloshing boiling water onto the ceiling and the walls. Seemingly hundreds of scalded roaches clacked to the floor, some dead, others scurrying to holes between the floor and the walls. I felt the color drain from my face, and I backed up to the window. Verdine and I watched as the woman climbed down.

I envied Verdine's composure as she took the woman's family census as thoroughly as any welfare worker, except that our primary purpose was to determine each family's spiritual status in the parish. Mrs. Torres was unmarried and had four children under age nine. We would give the pastor a detailed report, then use every means in our power to encourage her to attend weekly Mass and to have her children baptized, returning them to the Church's soul-saving sacraments. Our missionary purpose was to benefit our parishioners spiritually, first, before we attempted to relieve their desperate social conditions.

The moment I stepped back into the daylight, I dropped my skirts, shaking my habit vigorously. "This place isn't even fit for those creepy roaches," I complained, "let alone for human beings. How can they live here? How can they have a life that does not have the quality of God?"

Verdine nodded sadly, saying nothing; she frowned as she looked uneasily down the narrow street.

I went on, "This place stinks, stale water running down their halls. Did you see those broken pipes and . . ."

"Roseann . . . please!" Verdine said, her eyes widening at my outburst. " 'The poor you have always with you,' " she quoted from the Bible. "These conditions are part and parcel of being poor," she added feebly. "At least we can help them spiritually, and she picked up a faster pace down the street.

"But it's insane; they have dozens of kids and they're starving."

Sister Verdine glanced back at me. "Poor souls; they have no riches. All they have are their children." An edge underlined her tone.

I felt a pall descend on the joys of my recent final vows. Yesterday I'd worn a white crown. My heart and soul had feasted on the love of Jesus and on the tenderness of Father Barrett. My lungs had been filled with the sweet fragrance of roses and frankincense. Today, Harlem sickened me with the smell of decay, of misery; it was a troubling paradox, a slap in the face.

By the end of that morning we had arranged ten Baptisms, three First Communions, and the Catholic sacramental blessings on two common-law marriages. This should have rejoiced my heart and left me in peace, but it did not.

That evening as the chapel filled with Sisters to chant the Holy Office of the Virgin Mary before supper, I couldn't get Verdine's words out of my mind. "The poor you have always with you," not a consoling thought. Heat and fatigue lay heavily on me and I could hardly sing the Latin phrases. Half dozing, though I was kneeling, I found my heart with Father Barrett, asking for answers. There was a light tap on my shoulder. I looked up to see that the Sisters had started filing downstairs.

Sister Laura, the convent's Superior, sat at the head of the dining table next to old Sister Josepha, the last functional pioneer nun in the Congregation. She had cofounded the order with Mother Foundress, and although the order was changing, Sister Josepha was not. She read the Roman Martyrology in a droning voice, as the steaming pot roast was passed back and forth until the platter reached me at the foot of the table. I was served last as the youngest in age and lowest in religious rank.

Sister Laura and Sister Josepha made an interesting contrast. Sister Laura, in her mid-forties, was short and plump. Her colorless skin and whisper-soft voice seemed to deny the confidence she enjoyed as an experienced and competent Superior. Sister Josepha, who at seventy-eight was nearly twice her age, had once been tall and slender. Now, although her movements were slow and sometimes trembling, her voice was strong and expressed an alert and lively sense of humor.

As soon as Sister Laura whispered, "Let our conversation be modest, charitable, and truthful," opening recreation, I moved to sit with Sister Josepha. I had no heart to brag about my first day in the parish.

Sister Josepha's manner was somewhat abrupt. "Take these," she said, pressing a packet of tinted holy pictures into my hands.

In return, I took her hand, feeling a glow of warmth from our contact as her lips formed a half smile. I had loved this veteran nun ever since she had come to my defense when I was a postulant.

I'd been sweeping the dining room floor when a senior Sister I didn't recognize dug the end of her long, bony finger into my back. "You're the piggiest postulant I've ever smelled," she growled.

"I'm sorry," I had said then, although the urge to hit her with my broom was as close as my next breath.

"You're too young to be with us," she had added. "You won't make it through the novitiate, mark my words!"

"What is this I hear?"

We both looked back to see Sister Josepha, her deep brown eyes accusing my tormentor. "And who's given *you* the authority to correct this young postulant?"

The nun left us quickly and Sister Josepha consoled me with, "It's not that she doesn't like you." She smiled. "It's a matter of too much time spent in service to things that we cannot possibly change."

The following morning I was on my own. Verdine intercepted me before I left for the parish. "Keep alert," she said protectively. "When you go into those tenements, know where the exits are. Keep a lookout for familiar faces and for strangers. Just because we wear a religious habit doesn't mean we are always safe." I smiled. "And when you walk out of those apartments, be sure to look up. Someone might throw a chamber pot on your head. It's happened before."

An hour later I knocked at a splintered apartment door. "Who?" carried through the thin plywood.

"I'm Sister Roseann," I called back.

A tired-looking woman opened the door a crack until she saw my habit. "Ah . . . Sister," she said, allowing me to enter. I followed her into the kitchen and bedroom, past a foul smelling bathroom. I saw she had soaked some old sheets and hung them on hand-strung lines by the windows to cool her cramped quarters. Shriveling orange wallpaper stuck out despondently from the cracks, and old pie pans caught the drips from the broken pipes.

A young man rose from a rumpled cot. "Tell her to leave," he called out harshly, staring me down.

"You go, Manuel," she answered, waving her small fist in front of his scarred face.

A sneer formed on Manuel's lips. He took a comb from his pocket and slicked back his blue-black hair, muttering something in Spanish about me—something terrible, I was sure—before he kicked the door shut behind him.

"He's not really bad," apologized Mrs. Garcia. "I'm sorry for his ways . . ."

"Is he your oldest son . . . your oldest child?" I asked evenly.

The woman pulled at her hair. "Manuel is angry, always angry."

"But why is he angry at me?"

"He tells me the Church is rich, they don't care about poor people. The priests, they drive big cars, live in beautiful houses . . . he doesn't understand," she said, searching my eyes, expecting some answer.

I struggled to formulate one that would refute Manuel's charges, but his words had stung me. The Church rich? Yes, compared to this, it was. He had just cause but frightening little insight to guide him. "I want to help you, not just to get your children baptized. I want to help your son if I can, Mrs. Garcia."

She managed an obedient smile as she placed a steaming cup of black coffee before me. I was supposed to explain that we were not allowed to partake food outside of the convent, but I could not offend her hospitality. Certainly this was not the moment. Mrs. Garcia's head sunk over her coffee, her heavy breasts sagging onto her rounded stomach.

"When do you expect the baby to arrive?" I asked, trying to hide the pain I felt for her.

"Two months," she said, showing gapped yellow teeth against puffed, bleeding gums. The grayness of her face worried me, and I resisted the sudden urge to bite my nails. "Please . . . help my Manuel," she pleaded. "I don't want him in that gang. If he had a father, a good father, he'd listen . . ." Her voice became a whimper.

"I will, I will . . ." I said, taking her hand.

Outside, Manuel leaned against the banister.

"I'll see you when I visit your mother again," I said lightly, offering him my sweetest smile. He studied me sullenly.

Before I turned the corner, I glanced back to see him and two other boys, less than fifteen, it seemed, laughing and bouncing their fists off each other. A slight smile on Manuel's face eased its hardness. He was almost handsome. Arranging for the Baptisms of his three brothers and two sisters, for their First Communions, would be easy. Winning Manuel's trust was another matter.

Every home I visited for the rest of the afternoon complained of the Street Gents, of their robbing, terrorizing children, vandalizing property. Their parents, like Mrs. Garcia, had long since lost control. They ran wild, exhilarated with being bad, from the youngest member of twelve to the oldest of twenty. It was from their worried mothers that I discovered that Manuel Garcia was the gang's leader.

Two weeks passed. I visited several dozen more families making a point to see Mrs. Garcia every other day, watching her labor under the weight she carried on too frail a frame. I searched for Manuel, who deliberately eluded me. Verdine was working at the other end of the parish, and I felt unprotected.

One morning as I was coming from the Garcia apartment, I heard loud young voices drifting up from the basement of a crumbling tenement and I thought I recognized Manuel's voice. I hesitated, then crept down the basement stairs. It smelled of decay and I hit a foul pile of excrement with my shoe. The carcass of a dead cat lay near it. My insides contracted and I pressed my hands over my mouth.

The basement door was ajar. Inside, Manuel was confronting a half dozen young boys, drawing the tip of his thumb over the point end of an ice pick. "I lead here, *cabron!*" he yelled. Then he flicked the point over a boy's nose, drawing a trickle of blood. The boy did not move. The room was silent.

"Hey, man, I thought it was okay . . . honest, man," the boy whimpered.

"I do the thinking," Manuel said coldly. "You take orders."

I felt sick. I had to get away, get fresh air. As I started up the stairs, a small gray animal shot out in front of me. "Jesus," I called out, sweat prickling my face. An enormous rat skirted through a broken board. Pulling up my habit skirt, I was turning to run when a hand gripped my arm, stopping me.

"Looking for me?" Manuel looked back into the room. "Hey, you guys . . . *salgan, todos!*"

They tore up the basement stairs past me, the young boy holding his bloodied nose. I could hear them running down the street. Manuel and I were alone.

"Take your hands off me," I said steadily.

Manuel released me, but he stepped in front of me on the stairway. His mocking eyes never left me, seeming to take pleasure in his control.

"I've been hoping I could find you," I said, forcing a calm tone. "But we can talk on the street."

"We talk here." It dawned on me, crazily, that he had never called me Sister. I prayed to God, to every saint in heaven, that he wouldn't hurt me. "Your mother looks worse each time I visit her," I said. "The baby will come soon. You're the oldest! She needs medical care and your help with the children . . ."

A smile twisted one corner of his mouth. "She needs me? She always needs Manuel!" he said in a half-dance mimic of his mother's flighty walk. As he talked I moved slightly, positioning myself to run if given half a chance. I felt the blood pulsing in my legs. Jesus help me, I prayed.

"What do you *know* about me?" he shouted, suddenly backing off, pointing to his chest, not allowing my answer. "What the hell you looking for? I mean it, woman. What you *looking* for with me here?" He ripped open his shirt, seeming to dare me to look at his smooth, hard chest.

I sagged against the banister, weak with fear. I had to distract him, I thought frantically. "I'm here because I care . . .

care about your mother, your family, the people I visit in this parish, that's why I'm here."

Manuel's eyes narrowed. His wary look said that he had fought for survival from the moment he had been pulled from his mother's undernourished breast. A sense of helplessness swept through me in face of his hate. "Care?" he shoved his fist close to my eyes. "You don't give a damn. You come here for your kicks and you leave, just like my papa. It's no different. Your priests care we go to church to pay . . . pay . . . for fine houses . . . big cars. You'll leave us like all the rest." He laughed bitterly. "Babies? Puerto Rican babies," he shouted, "are food for Harlem's rats, like the widow Martinez," and he swung his fist in a wide arc of anger in front of my face.

I moved back quickly. "Don't you *move*, woman!" The veins bulged in his neck. "You hear me."

I froze, obedient. Jesus . . . God, what possessed me to come down here . . . forgive me . . . help me, I begged Him.

"Martinez, she live two apartments down the hall. When she asleep, a rat ate the wool in her baby's mattress. It ate her baby's ear off! Its eyes! . . . its guts. You hear that, woman?" he yelled. "Babies are for damn rats!"

"Manuel . . . please . . . listen . . ."

"The hell I will!" he spat. "Fuck you . . . fuck your church . . . fuck God!"

"I don't care what you think," I said. "As long as I walk these streets, I am trying to do something! *Something!*" My own anger was dissolving all consideration of prudence. Bracing myself, I turned from him and started slowly up the stairs, not daring to look around, chastising myself. I had intruded into Manuel's "turf," as he called it. I was not to be trusted. My God, he could have raped me, killed me, but he hadn't. Lord, you are my Protector, my Shield, I prayed.

I dragged myself to the bus stop, hoping Verdine would be there waiting for me. I should think of Manuel as an animal, get to know how an animal's mind worked, I told myself, then hated myself for thinking of him as less than human.

"Roseann, you look terrible. What happened?"

Then it burst—the fear, the anger, the resentment, the absolute mortification of spirit and soul that I had undergone—but I could not tell her everything. I could not tell her that almost as intense as my fear had been my painful, shameful awareness of Manuel's masculinity. I dared not. I had been scared to death and the tears of release felt good. "Manuel hates his mother, hates me, hates the Church. He hates God . . . hates himself . . ."

♥ 4 ♥

We were almost through our summer assignment before we visited Saint Ann's pastor. Father John Jason had just returned, refreshed from his annual retreat in the Adirondacks. Verdine sat on the edge of the stuffed chair in the rectory office. We carried sixty case cards abbreviating each family's spiritual status in exact, precise terms, all neatly filed in a shoe box with the census cards according to streets and apartments.

Father Jason finally entered, patting his thinning hair, and sat down behind his oak desk, sliding back considerably to accommodate a well-rounded middle. "I'm pleased with your work, Sisters," he said as he thumbed through the cards.

"Father," Verdine interrupted, "I am working on a sewing project for some of the young girls. We need money for material—and for a used sewing machine," Verdine added tactfully.

"Money? Where do you suppose we're going to get it?" Father Jason barked. "How much?"

"Fifty dollars . . . to get started."

Jason tapped his stubby fingers on his desk.

"There must be a way, Father," Verdine said less calmly.

"Do you realize, Sister, that poor people don't support our parish? If it wasn't for our religious order, this place would be on the shelf. You'd think the Archbishop would divert a few pennies from the rich parishes," he added bitterly. He pushed back his chair and stood up, indicating that our visit was at an end. Slowly, he dug into his pocket and pulled out some green bills. "This might help a bit," he said, not looking at us. He shoved the bills into Verdine's hand and exited quickly.

"How much?" I asked eagerly as Verdine totaled the fives and tens. "Praise the Lord. Seventy dollars. Exactly what I needed! Just couldn't bring myself to ask for more, that's all."

"The reward of faith," I said, feeling keenly the failure of my own faith.

The busy summer weeks were passing quickly. One morning I spotted Sister Josepha walking with small and faltering steps on her way to Saint Ann's rectory. "Want a companion?" I asked cheerfully, lightly touching the seam of her sleeve.

Josepha took my hand, and my mood grew brighter. "I've noticed less smiles from your pretty young face these past days," she said.

"It's just that I haven't been able to accomplish my goals." I found myself biting on a cuticle. Before I knew it, I was pouring out every detail. "I know I should be more concerned for the families' spiritual welfare, but . . ." I added contritely.

"Saith who?" Josepha asked in a mildly mocking chirp. "Our beloved Foundress always taught her Sisters that we must attempt to ease the social and material burdens of the poor," she added reverently, "for how can they listen receptively to the word of God if their bellies are empty, if they are in rags? Only when their social ills have been relieved will true healing of the spirit take place." Josepha's eyes were clouded with memories.

Her steps became slower as she spoke. "Healing rises in our hearts, from the outpouring of our love, from the love we have for Jesus. It is then that the healing energy pours forth . . . invisible to the eye, but no less powerful. Look to Jesus, our Teacher, our Healer, the One who touched lepers. He is the example, for you, for me, to continue His work, not just the Apostles . . ."

As she spoke I was struck by her intensity and by the memory of Father Barrett's words, different words, but the same message. If only we could return to the convent and talk, I thought as she squeezed my hand.

"I just want to die with my boots on," she said simply and unexpectedly. I watched her pause after every step to take several short breaths as she made her way up the rectory stairs.

"Were you going to ask something?" Josepha asked, turning back.

I hesitated for a moment. "Do you know Father Barrett's address? I want to thank him for his wonderful retreat . . ." I couldn't go on. I knew rightfully well that if Mother Edmond had wanted us to have access to Barrett for spiritual counsel, his address would have been posted.

Old Sister Josepha looked at me over her glasses. "Father Barrett is a marvel, a holy man." Her face lit up. "I'll put his address in your office book this afternoon. When you write, tell him I pray for him every day." Then she added, under her breath, "God knows he needs our prayers." She entered the rectory, and I felt a sudden heaviness out of keeping with our sharing.

Very late that afternoon the Motherhouse's official car was parked in front of the convent. Verdine quickly waved me to the side parlor. "This morning Sister Josepha went to God."

I sank into the sofa chair, unwilling to believe what she had said. "What?"

"Apparently, she had been sitting for a while before Father Jason found her slumped over in the rectory chair. He administered the Last Rites. She died the way she had always wanted to die," Verdine added thoughtfully.

"With her boots on," I said, still dazed. "That's what she told me this morning, as if she'd had a premonition . . ."

Verdine's hand moved gently toward me and slowly she drew it back.

I began to weep.

"You must control yourself, Roseann," she said softly. "This is not the time for grief or tears. It is a time to rejoice in Josepha's eternal reward."

When I had gained some control over my tears, I sat in the back of the chapel beside Josepha's kneeler, staring at her prayer books. The sitting pad she kept there had already been removed. She had never returned to the convent to give me Father Barrett's address. The tears began again. "I will miss you, my friend, my dear Josepha."

That night Mother Edmond sat at the head of the table. She approached me after the meal. "Have you enjoyed your summer assignment?" she asked in a low voice, her eyes fastened on me searchingly.

"I have," I said simply.

"Keep up God's good work," she said, turning back to the room.

I edged my way toward the door, glancing at Sister Josepha's favorite corner, already occupied. Would Josepha be forgotten as quickly as her corner had been taken? I wondered sadly.

Her body was placed in a plain black coffin in the chapel's nave. Each of the Sisters took turns praying for the repose of her soul. " 'Yea, though I walk through the valley of the shadow of death, I will fear no evil; for thou art with me; thy rod and thy staff comfort me.' "

I took my place before the coffin, watching her still, peaceful body. She had smiled upon me and held my hand for the last time only hours before. For a long time no words of my own came to me. "Help me, Sister Josepha," I prayed. I buried my head in my hands until there were no more tears, only the aching in my ribs. The lines in Sister Josepha's old face were sweetly eased in death, and a white crown of roses rested gently on her head. The long cross of ebony, the symbol of our final vows, was set between her stiff, cold fingers. "Unless you wear my crown of thorns, Sister Roseann, you cannot wear my eternal Crown of Glory," came from Jesus in the tabernacle. In that moment I did not want to embrace His words. It hurt too much.

Sister Josepha's funeral was crowded with priests, mostly young, and the parishioners she had served faithfully for forty years. Father Jason preached the sermon. He talked of how with her passing went the last link to our Mother Foundress. Sister Josepha had cofounded our religious Order back in the 1920s. Specializing in the missionary visitation of families as social workers had been a radical departure from the usual religious orders of teaching and nursing nuns.

"It wasn't easy in those early days," Josepha had said more than once. "The Church tested our community of women. We walked the streets of the poor alone, but we proved ourselves capable. We won the approval of Mother Church."

Father Jason praised her. "Sister Josepha died to herself through her holy vows and gave the fullness of her life and of her gifts to the service of Christ and to His Church. This precious legacy she leaves for all of you, courageous enough to imitate her."

Mother Edmond rose, her eyes lowered, and we followed her graceful movements. She closed Josepha's casket, sealed forever.

Sister Verdine genuflected beside me and whispered, "I have news for you." We stepped outside the chapel. Her eyes were dark. "You knew your assignment here would soon be over. Your new Superior, Sister Maurice, just phoned. She wants you to return to Ronston tomorrow morning."

I leaned heavily against the wall. "No. It's too soon. I have work yet to do. Manuel has been opening up to me lately; he said he'd see me tomorrow . . . we could talk . . . I promised him. He won't understand. Believe me, I must see him. It's what I've been working for. Please!"

Verdine stiffened. "Sister Roseann, listen to me. It is the holy will of God that you return to your own mission. He speaks through the will of your Superiors. Christ will give you special grace for unquestioning obedience."

I remembered much the same message, word for word, that she had repeated so many times when I was her postulant. It was this message of obedience and submission that was the root and substance of my religious life, the ideals of my final vows. She left me alone, and I returned to kneel before Sister Josepha's coffin.

Before I left Saint Joseph's Convent the next morning with my one suitcase, I found Verdine waiting at the door. "God bless you, Roseann. You did wonderful work with me in Harlem." She held my hands tightly. "And I wish you a holy and fruitful year in Ronston."

"Thank you, Sister," I said, unable to hide my anxiety. "Please. Please see Manuel. Explain what happened about my transfer. Promise me . . ."

Manuel had told me that I would leave him, like all the rest had, like his papa.

ST. MARY'S CONVENT
Ronston, New Jersey

♉ 5 ♉

The bus wound its way to New Jersey. Each time I closed my eyes, I saw Sister Josepha's casket being lowered into a cement box and sealed in the cold earth at the Motherhouse cemetery. Only a small white wooden cross would mark the place. Would my place be by the old oak tree near the first Station of the Cross, where I usually dove into the green pinewoods to run? Would I die an old nun?

I had been on a teaching assignment in Ronston for the year before my final vows. Now I was returning to an old assignment, but with a new Superior, Sister Maurice, who had insisted I be taken from my summer assignment five days early. Her decision still angered me. The ten summer weeks away from my mission at Ronston had seemed more like ten years. I had no choice now but to focus on the harsh reality of the work that awaited me.

The local bus deposited me in front of the convent, a large white Victorian house gracing a hillside opposite the gentle Ronston River. It was a beautiful old house, solid and secure, chosen for the Sisters four years earlier by Father Dweyer, after he'd visited the convent the Sisters had lived in for some twenty years. "It's not fit for humans, much less nuns," he had told Bishop Neal. I had heard that old Father

Briam had a fit when Father Dweyer took over the renovation project and presented him a bill for fifty thousand dollars. Father Briam was dead three months, and I remembered Father Barrett's words: "He died of a heart attack, Roseann. It had nothing to do with the fact that you spoke your mind." I smiled to myself.

Sister Maurice greeted me. "You look remarkably healthy, Sister Roseann," she said, almost too eagerly, it seemed. "We need young blood in our convent." I smiled with enormous effort. "Unpack and then I'd like to see you in my office." Maurice walked back into the kitchen, issuing cooking instructions to rosy-faced Sister Judith, a former Brooklyn convent Superior.

Quietly, I passed through two large parlors where leaded French windows gathered the sunshine. The furniture had been moved since I was last here, indicating that Maurice had begun to imprint her personal preferences as Superior. I loved these parlors and their sense of the old. Often I imagined beautiful women and handsome men dancing gracefully here a century before.

When I genuflected at the chapel door, I recognized Sister Gerald, who had first cut my hair as a postulant. She had given in to my pleas that day and cut my hair below my ears in spite of the cummunity custom to cut it shorter. Since that time, I had felt a special fondness for her.

My tiny attic bedroom was suffocating, the heat overpowering in the absence of a fan. Maurice, I hoped, would be more merciful than my former Superior, who had insisted I keep my bedroom door closed.

Hurriedly, I threw my clothes into the dresser and gathered my mail, pulling out letters from Eileen. I was starved for news from home.

Maurice appeared at the doorway. "Leave your personal business until after our conference," she said in a tone that seemed self-conscious of her new authority.

Her desk was arranged in absolute order and she sat stiffly behind it, leaving me standing before her for several min-

utes. The view from that position exaggerated her long, thin
nose. Everything about her was thin, sharply and angularly
thin. I guessed that she was forty or fifty years old; with Sister Maurice it was hard to tell. She had a thin dry cough
which seemed to come from her throat rather than her chest.
It became more noticeable when she was exercising her
position as Superior. She did not lower her eyes in the customary gesture, but instead, turned her face slightly to the
left as if to look past me rather than at me.

She coughed. "You may take a chair. You've heard, I'm
sure, Roseann, that Father Dweyer has been appointed new
pastor of St. Mary's," she offered.

"I'm not surprised," I said.

"It is my understanding that our Sisters have poor reputa-
tions as teachers and as disciplinarians in all of the parish's
catechetical centers," she said, leaning forward. I thought of
a cat ready to pounce.

"Perhaps, Sister, but there are reasons," I answered. "We
are forced to teach in crowded, cold churches. We have no
teaching aids. We use outdated and boring catechisms. We
each carry the workload of five, and don't ask me how
many hours we spend on the road transporting children
home. It takes its toll, Sister," I added, pulling at the white
collar sticking to my neck.

"I'm aware of the hardships, Roseann, but regardless,
there is no reason for lack of order. None." She looked at
me as if I were to blame for the standards she felt had been
violated.

Hardships? I thought of Manuel and his pathetic mother
and her soon-to-be-born baby living in a couple of rat- and
roach-infested rooms. The thought of Manuel left me with a
deep and aching pain. Yes, I could handle hardships, but I
rebelled at the idea of hardships that didn't have to be even
more than at hardships that seemed inevitable.

Sister Maurice's voice seemed to soften. "I'll need your
help until I'm familiar with the routine."

"Of course," I answered dutifully, wondering if my best

would be good enough. I took my time detailing the all too familiar teaching schedules of our one thousand public school children. She never asked me to repeat a thing, not even the most complex work situations.

"You've been in charge of St. Mary's teaching program?" she asked. I nodded. She rose from her chair, facing me. "It's too much responsibility for any junior Sister, especially with a new pastor such as Father Dweyer, demanding as he is."

The soles of my feet grew hot. "I've managed well enough under old Father Briam and he wasn't the easiest pastor to work for." There was a quick moment of recognition in Maurice's eyes, recognition of my ability to fence with her. As arrogant as it was, I thought I detected a small note of admiration.

"I've been told you've done a remarkable job. Still, less responsibility will benefit your spiritual development. You will be my assistant at St. Mary's, of course." There was something final in her manner. "We have our first rectory appointment with Father Dweyer tomorrow morning. It's important we make a good impression." I stared at her. Good impression meant she would do the talking. My role was to be silent—very, very silent.

I left her office emotionally drained and retreated to my room with my precious mail. For the good of my spiritual life? What could a new Superior possibly know about my spiritual life? Then the curtain began to lift. Mother Edmond knew, and Mother Edmond had groomed Sister Maurice for this assignment.

During my first recreation period I felt my youth keenly compared to these five senior nuns, older both in years and in the religious life. Sister Clara mumbled to herself, but no one paid much attention since she was near seventy. Sister Gerald smiled at me frequently and I looked forward to teaching with her. As we strolled our half acre of cherry trees and weeping willows, I swatted at the mosquitoes that swarmed up from the river bed and moved closer to Sister Judith, attracted by her easy warmth and humor.

"Will I be working with you, bright eyes?" Judith asked playfully.

No nun had ever called me by a nickname and never so endearingly. "Bright eyes?" I asked.

"Indeed," Judith said. "It does fit you."

I looked directly at Sister Judith. Although she could not be described as pretty, she was plump and pleasant-looking, with a round, soft warmth about her. For some reason, even though there was no physical resemblance, she made me think of my mother. Here, in this fragrant but humid orchard, Sister Judith fanned herself with the short shoulder cape of her habit, delightfully unaware that this might not be considered particularly dignified, smiling in the pleasant relief of the small breeze she was creating. Sister Maurice watched from a distance with Sister Lorene, a fat, placid, middle-aged nun, at her side. The other Sisters joined us, drawn like bees to the honeycomb that Judith seemed to be.

During prayers that night, a lightness swept me up as I listened to Judith read the evening meditation. She made me feel secure. In spite of tomorrow's uncertain visit with Father Dweyer and Maurice's expectations, I slept well.

While we waited in Father Dweyer's office, I was reminded of the reputation he was bringing to St. Mary's. He had left Sacred Heart, the leading parish in the diocese, where both young and old flocked from other parishes, to the dismay of their pastors, to hear his sermons and, without a doubt, to feast their eyes on his finely chiseled features. He was a man used to getting his way, I'd heard, especially with Bishop Neal.

Sister Maurice coughed dryly and asserted her authority quickly, updating Father Dweyer on our catechetical and family visitation program without a flaw. She amazed me.

Father Dweyer patiently bided his time, then leaned forward in his chair. "Sisters, Father Briam's administration of this parish oozes from neglect . . . decay . . . and Briam's incompetence." Disdain edged his voice, and I thought that I would never want to cross this man.

"In a few months, Sisters, you won't recognize this parish." His lips curved as he paused, observing our silence. "Father Johnson, my former assistant, has replaced Father Carson. He's the best curate any pastor could work with and we'll be starting the building fund drive at the end of this month for the new elementary school and convent." Father Dweyer's eyes had grown enormously brighter and his energy bounced about the office as he drummed his fingers avidly on the desk top. Without a doubt, St. Mary's would be rebuilt in his own image and likeness.

"I am pleased with your projections for a modern parish," Sister Maurice offered calmly, "but there are a few things I feel must be changed."

"Oh?" He smiled and leaned back in his chair.

"Please understand that our missionary work does not include church ironing, training and recruiting altar boys, cleaning the church, or counting Sunday collections. This is the work of janitors, church sacristans, and priests."

"But, Sister, haven't you noticed I've stopped all that in my parish? However, if you have trouble with the other three pastors, please inform me. I pay most of the bills around here; I don't anticipate any problems."

Sister Maurice smiled warmly. "Thank you for your understanding. May we have your blessing?" Our knees hit the floor as Father Dweyer benevolently raised his hand, blessing us both.

"Father Dweyer and I will make a fine team," Maurice said later, her face radiant in anticipation.

I felt I would have no part in this cozy relationship, but I admired Maurice for speaking up. The Sisters had become work horses because many Superiors had been too spineless to reject the unreasonable demands of pastors.

Father Edwards passed us in the rectory hallway and laughed. "Robbed the cradle, have you?" he said, grinning and pointing to me.

Maurice smiled indulgently.

"I assure you, Father, I am not a child," I answered quickly.

He laughed harder, and I felt instant dislike for Father Dweyer's youngest assistant.

"Don't take it so personally, Roseann," Sister Maurice said. "You look seventeen, not twenty-two. One day you'll be so old you won't remember being young." She laughed companionably.

Seven weeks into the teaching program, I started visiting the families of troublesome children in my classes. Some roads led to affluent, brick-walled estates, but most homes in St. Mary's were lived in by modest middle-class families. However, all of them were pleasant now, in the clean first winter snowfall.

I was waiting for Mrs. Evans to come back into the living room when I caught sight of the picture in the newspaper on the low table in front of me. I stared at the photo of a scarred-faced boy with dark wavy hair. Manuel Garcia was handcuffed between two policemen. "Taken forcefully," it read, "into custody for first-degree murder . . . gang killing."

As Mrs. Evans came into the room, I fought for control. "I'm afraid I don't feel well. I'll return tomorrow, Mrs. Evans."

Back at the convent, I pulled myself heavily up to my attic room, passing Judith dusting the staircase. She looked up and reached out to me with one urgent gesture. This small act of concern broke the wall that had been holding back my tears. Sobbing, I fell across my bed.

Judith was there beside me, stroking my shoulders. "What has happened, Roseann?" she asked softly.

The story of Manuel poured out. "It's just that I feel I could have done more. I failed Manuel somehow. I failed him. Verdine told me my obedience, my submission to God's will, could be the source of Manuel's conversion . . . and he's killed someone . . . murdered."

"Roseann." Judith took my shoulders firmly and gently turned me to face her, now stroking my forehead and pushing back my veil. "You must believe you gave the best you had to give to Manuel under the circumstances. You're far harder on yourself than the good Lord intends. Manuel might have listened to you, but I doubt it. You can't save the whole suffering world. Even St. Paul, as great as he was, couldn't be all things to all of mankind. It's a cross you must learn to carry."

"But if I had kept my word, seen him, it might have saved Manuel. I let him down . . . like everyone he had ever allowed himself to trust."

"Roseann, it's not given for us to understand *all* the mysteries of life, of death, of misery, or the complexities of human existence. It would drive us to madness. When you pray for Manuel's soul, put his spiritual welfare into God's merciful hands . . . in faith. Release him from your mind in peace. You must learn to let go, otherwise you'll wrinkle like a prune, grow old and sickly. God knows we have enough sick nuns in our community."

I could hear Father Barrett's voice. Beloved old Josepha had once renewed his message. Now Judith was doing it again for me. I realized that I had thought of Josepha as a friend in spite of the difference in our ages! Josepha had been my first and only friend in the Order, even though friendships among the Sisters were not encouraged. Now Judith was offering that special gift. Through my terrible pain for Manuel, I felt a glow of gratitude.

As I listened to Judith's soothing voice, I suddenly became aware that we were alone, alone in my bedroom, talking, something we were not allowed. Instantly, she seemed to read my mind.

"Don't worry yourself. If we cannot help each other in times like this, our religious lives become the empty shells of hermit crabs." It was the first time I wished myself old. Only age could be the golden vessel of wisdom, tested and polished by the grace of long years.

❦ 6 ❦

At the time, I never would have believed that the pain I felt for Manuel would diminish enough to bear. But suddenly it was spring, the busiest time of the school year with Confirmations and First Communions. On a beautiful spring day, I spotted a long white envelope addressed in my mother's familiar script. It always gave me a sense of excitement.

> *Dear Elizabeth,*
> *Our old friend Howard died blissfully at the age of ninety-five, leaving me some money—just enough to visit you next week. It's the only time I can take from the law tests, which are way past deadlines. Only wish old Howard had passed on a few months earlier; I'd have been able to be with you on your day of final vows . . .*

I ran into Sister Maurice's office, waving my letter excitedly. "My mother's coming. I can't believe it . . . seven years . . ."

Maurice did not look up from her paperwork. "I know," she said flatly. She had read my letter, as was the community custom for our Superiors. "It's a pity she comes when we're so pressed with work."

"But it's the only time she can come. Certainly under the circumstances we can be flexible," I said irritably.

With her familiar gesture, she turned her face to the left and looked past me. She coughed dryly. "I can't relieve you of your assignments. You'll just have to manage."

I stomped out of her office. My stomach felt pinched; I wanted my mother to be treated like a queen. Was it so vain of me to want my mother to feel proud of me?

I parked the community car outside the Darson Hotel, a grand place in the early 1900s, waiting for my mother's bus to arrive from the airport. I was only a few weeks away from my twenty-third birthday and I wondered what my mother would think of me now that we had been separated since I was sixteen. Mothers don't change, I told myself . . . but their children grow up.

I realized that I was holding my breath as I watched the passengers emerge slowly from the silver-gray bus. There she was. Her shiny black hair was turning gray. She looked remarkably beautiful, something I had never fully appreciated when I was growing up. As we kissed and hugged, I smelled the forgotten scent of her, rushing childhood feelings back so fast I felt dizzy.

She was still tall and slender, but in the intervening seven years I had grown an inch or so taller than she. I pulled back to look at her. She still carried herself with proud grace, and now, her eyes were moist with tears. I suddenly realized how grateful I was for those tears, how much I wanted this beautiful and familiar stranger to let me know that she loved me. I held her hand as we walked to the rear of the bus to get her luggage.

We left her bags at Mrs. Sebanski's, where I had arranged a room for her, and drove to the convent.

"Picture-book house," Mother remarked as Sister Maurice greeted her briefly.

"Thank God you had a safe trip," she answered dryly. "I

know both of you have a lot to catch up with." She exited quickly out the back parlor.

I left Mother alone during prayers, and I could smell her cigarette smoke when I returned. How would she react when I told her how precious little time I would be permitted to spend with her? Regardless, I thought, I would take her with me everywhere I could.

She was resting comfortably in the parlor when I brought in the tray with her dinner. "Aren't you going to eat with me, Bussy?" It had been a long time since I had heard this pet name.

"We're not permitted to dine except with the Sisters. It's one of our customs."

"And one of the stupidest, I'm sure," she fired back. "I am your mother. Doesn't that make a difference?"

"I'm afraid it doesn't."

She drummed her fork irritably on the plate. "And why can't I stay with you here in the convent? Most religious orders provide a guest room for parents." Her dark eyes narrowed in disappointment. Trying to explain our many rules and strange customs would be a waste of time with my mother. She would demand logical, sensible explanations, her wits refined as a law editor and her worldly experience tested in daily survival.

"Maybe someday, Mother, we'll have more privileges," I said lightly.

"Do you think your Order will permit you to come home for Eileen's wedding?"

I shook my head sadly. She was intimidating me by these questions and her disappointment. I had wanted my mother to be pleased and happy with my life, but every time I opened my mouth, I seemed to offend her.

She had been with me barely two days and I could feel her withdrawing. "You've changed so, Elizabeth. You seem so . . . so controlled, so detached," she said with a sad face while we walked through the nearby pasture fields. Her words stunned me. We said nothing for what seemed a long time.

"What do you mean, changed?"

"Oh, it's so many things." She busied herself with her camera. Mother wasn't a person lost for words, and I knew she had chosen not to explain. Maybe she was afraid of hurting my feelings, but I felt wounded enough as it was. If my twin sister could have come, our visit might have been different, easier perhaps. Painfully, I had to admit to myself that our separation had taken a heavy toll. My mother no longer knew me as she once had. I couldn't bring myself to pursue the subject, afraid of answers I might not want to hear.

"And do you like being a law editor?" I asked when she remained silent.

"A job is a job," she said, adding with a smile, "lawyers are helpless without legal secretaries. But with my work it's a point of celebration when any attorney pays his bills."

I laughed. Mother was sharper than I remembered, more critical, and now I felt I was losing her.

Then without warning she asked, "Are you *really* happy being a nun? I mean, does it satisfy you?"

For a moment I couldn't think. "Mother, you've seen me teach, visit the families . . . Of course I love my life, my work."

"That's not what I mean. Your life with these nuns, enduring imprisoning rules?"

"I wouldn't be here if I didn't love my religious life."

She seemed not to hear. "It's never too late, to come home, Elizabeth. It won't be a disgrace. You can go to college, get a good job, get married, have a family. Listen, there is so much living, so much good you can accomplish without having to renounce the world for the rest of your life. Consider what you've done as a tour . . . of . . . of service. Like in the military."

I pushed away from her. "Is that why you've come?"

"Honey, of course not. I'm your mother. I want the best for you. You've had enough time to live out this austere life. You're older now! Wiser!" Her eyes searched mine for bare truth and I knew she was not satisfied.

"My life of prayer, of faith, can work miracles," I said bravely.

"Miracles!" She laughed almost derisively. "At the Shrine of Lourdes, where millions of the faithful crawl on their knees in hope, prayers dropping from their lips, how many first-rate miracles of lasting healing take place? In spite of the prayers of the Catholic Church?" She shook her head. "It's what takes place, my dear, in one's heart that heals, regardless of religion. And the Church condemns even its own living saints, in particular those who try to liberate the mind. I am thinking of the Jesuit Teilhard De Chardin." She smiled faintly. "I always admired his ideas on the 'energy of evolution,' but the Church silenced him."

I was feeling shaky. I didn't remember my mother ever speaking with such forcefulness. "I have never heard of him," I said.

"Pity your religious Order doesn't care to educate you," she replied sharply.

"Someday they will. I know they will." I hated being on the defensive and I was no match for her.

"My dear," she said, "I'm not angry with you. But I am looking for something, something you *used* to have." I couldn't understand the intensity of her concern, and I strained to be cheerful in spite of my emotions. We had precious little time left to be with each other and the moments we spent together had become painful. I could not bring myself to ask her what she thought I had lost.

Mother and I said little on the way to the bus in spite of the many unspoken things still between us. "Do you think you'll come back to visit me again?" I asked.

"We'll see what the future holds," she replied in a noncommittal tone, one I remembered too well. That certain lack of inflection meant . . . no. *For all the days of my life*

. . . that had been my vow. Was this one short week all that I would ever have of my mother for all the days of my life? Although the adult face I showed to the world was dry-eyed, the child in my heart wept.

As the bus pulled into its loading lane, I clung to her, storing the memory of her touch and the security of her embrace.

She kissed me lightly, patting my veiled head. "Ah, my dear honey, my little grown-up girl!" She slipped quickly out of my arms into the bus and I lost her behind the smoked-glass windows.

❦ 7 ❦

My mother's visit had changed something in me. For the first time I was aware of a vague soul-deep restlessness. I still refused to look at the questions she had raised, but now I sometimes caught myself watching me and the other nuns around me as if I were both actress and audience for some strange exotic film. In those moments my role as a nun seemed less real than my role as observer.

In the week after my mother left, we finished the school year's religious classes. I observed my sixth-grade boys watching me as I instructed them on their Confirmation questions and answers. More than a few gazed at me dreamily. I had become accustomed to their longing looks, to their young sensitive feelings. I remembered Father Barrett's remarks on why I preferred teaching boys to girls, but I feared now that my enjoyment of them grew with every class. For the thousandth time I wondered where Father Barrett was, if he ever thought of me, if he ever kissed another nun's hands. Now more than ever I felt the need of his guidance, his consolation.

In moments like this, I tried to feel especially close to Jesus. If only I could see His face as had some of His saints. It was an idle dream, this wanting to walk with Him and feel the touch of His skin, a consolation not given to sinners. How many times I had been told that my life of faith was more pleasing to Christ, a truer test of my devotion, than the consolation of visions.

With summer and the end of the school year came our annual retreat at the Motherhouse. This was another reminder of Father Barrett; it was the anniversary of my kneeling before him to take my final vows. Just before I left for retreat, Sister Maurice offered me a slim volume of St. John of the Cross, known for his rare heights of mysticism.

"Read these," she said importantly, and coughed. "I don't give them just to anyone."

"St. John of the Cross? The dark night of the soul? But, Sister, I don't feel this is a book I need."

"I'll be the judge of that, Roseann. Read a few pages every day, but show them to no one."

I nodded, mystified, admitting to a glow of pride from her unusual demonstration of confidence in me. Carefully, I placed the book in the bottom of my suitcase along with my notes from Father Barrett's Retreat of the Smiling Faces, which had become frayed and fragile.

At the Motherhouse, Judith approached me by the tangled raspberry vines at the far edge of the garden where I hid to read. "Ah ha! So Maurice has decided to mold you according to Maurice."

"I don't understand what you mean," I said, puzzled.

"One piece of advice, Roseann. Be careful of Maurice, Superior or no Superior. Stick to the basics of spirituality." She walked on down the path, fanning herself with her shoulder cape. I closed the book.

What was she talking about? Admittedly, the readings of St. John disturbed me. I didn't want to understand the dark night of total surrender, of naked detachment with which he had been tormented. Father Barrett had exhorted us to a life of peace and joy in Christ and in our religious life. That's what I was striving for. It was what I had consecrated my life to achieving. And my reward would be the hundredfold eternal happiness.

When I arrived back in Ronston after the retreat, my body had erupted with ugly patches of red, driving me to frenzied scratching. I finally went to Sister Maurice. I hadn't yet reached the much-admired stage of enduring physical sufferings. "Look at my arms," I said, pulling up my sleeves. "What's wrong? I can't stand it any longer." I was unable to control my panic.

"Poison oak," she said calmly, unlocking the medicine cabinet. "Take this . . . it should help in a few days."

"Few days?" I tore at the patches of raised skin, drawing blood.

"I'll help you put it on," she offered.

"I can manage." I ran to the attic bathroom, where I ripped off my wool habit, bathing myself frantically with the lotion. When I faced the small mirror, I backed away shocked. I looked like a paste monster. Ugly! Ugly! Why would Maurice want to touch me? Sadly, I remembered the tanned, sound body with which I once had been so familiar. Since I had become a nun, I had never really looked at my body, except at my face, to adjust my veil.

It took seven days before the treatment worked, an eternity of itching. I tried to identify with the suffering Jesus, His garments sticking to His tender body when He had carried His cross. Willingly He had accepted His suffering, for love. Ashamed of my weakness, I prayed that my pain would end.

When I returned the lotion to Sister Maurice, she waved me into her bedroom. "Let me see if the scabs are completely gone. Take off your habit," she said.

I hesitated, then dropped my habit limply to her bedroom floor.

"Take off your underwear"—and she proceeded to peel it off, before I had lifted my hands.

Her fingers moved over my back slowly, sending chills through my body. I hated her touching me, looking at me naked, and for the first time in my life I felt ugly shame.

"Your back looks fine." She moved in front of me, staring long at my upper legs, at my stomach, at my breasts. She half smiled. "You've gotten over the poison oak faster than I did four years ago. You can put on your clothes." She helped button up my underwear, slowly flicking her fingers lightly against my breast.

I hurried upstairs and ran the bath water, soaking my body longer than the prescribed ten minutes. Why had she taken off my underwear? Why had she touched my body? Was it only an accident? This troubled me for days.

The following morning, Maurice stopped me in the kitchen. She asked, "Have you gained spiritual understanding from the readings of St. John?" Her face seemed brighter than usual.

"It confuses me," I said simply. "If you don't mind, I want to return it."

"And you wonder why your spiritual progress has been so slow, Roseann." I was silent. She patted her shoulder cape flat in front. "I am releasing you from St. Mary's parish and offering you to St. Thomas's parish. It's much smaller and it will give you more time to develop your spiritual life."

"But I'm under much less pressure than I've been in the past four years," I said hoarsely.

"It's for your own good!" She left abruptly, without further discussion.

I knew Father Dweyer liked me, and Father Johnson and I worked well together with St. Mary's family cases. My religious instruction classes were making fine progress. It didn't make sense.

I burst in on Judith, who was in the basement sorting out her visual teaching aids. "Maurice just pulled me out of St. Mary's for my so-called spiritual good! Why?"

"Best not ask me, Roseann."

"I'm asking. Tell me . . . please!" That I was breaking the rule of silence, of unnecessary conversation, was lost in my anger.

Judith's eyebrows knitted into sharp arrows. "It's against my better judgment."

"*Tell me!*"

"Okay, but you'll regret asking. I feel Maurice's motivations aren't entirely spiritual," she offered tentatively. I rested heavily against the cool cement wall. "You're too much in demand at St. Mary's. It's a matter, shall we say, of too much popularity for you and not enough for Maurice. Of course she'd say it might make you conceited and proud." Judith laughed.

"I can't believe that."

"Believe it, Roseann. You asked and I'm telling you. She's a deceptively jealous woman. You have been naïve not to recognize she must be the queen bee, she must have it all. I know her. We go back long years."

"You're wrong this time, Judith."

I was disturbed. This was not like Judith, with her usual good-humored warmth. I was sorry I had insisted that she tell me what she thought, what she would have kept silent if I had not demanded it. Had I hurt her somehow in forcing her to choose between her friendship to me and her loyalty to a Superior?

Several evenings later, I was making my holy hour of prayer in the chapel, absorbed with a book on Mother Stuart's life lent to me by Judith. I felt Sister Maurice touch my shoulder.

"Who gave you that book?"

I looked up. Her face was sharper than usual. "Judith. It's wonderful, I mean this woman founding a religious order much like our own Foundress, and . . ."

She hit the book to the floor, then genuflected and stomped out of the chapel.

I sat stunned for a few minutes, picked up the book, and followed out. At her office door I heard angry voices.

"I've seen you and Roseann huddle together at recreations . . . whispering . . . always whispering. Roseann is under *my* supervision, under *my* spiritual direction, Sister Judith!"

"How righteously you wear authority!" Judith said, her voice tense. "You're trying to mold Roseann into something she is not. You have no right to forbid us to share with each other. It's nonsense. Nonsense!"

"It is the Holy Rule. Personal friendships are forbidden." Maurice was shouting now.

"It's your rule! Your jealousy! That's why you took Roseann out of St. Mary's. Well, Father Dweyer will demand her back and you won't say boo."

"I'll have you transferred, Judith. I'll tell Mother Edmond you're undermining my authority. *My authority* is the will of God."

"Oh really? Mother Edmond knows me well, woman. You'll look like an ass."

I could hear Judith's footsteps heavy with anger on the back stairs. In her office, Maurice was kicking her file cabinets. I hid Judith's book in my closet and sat quietly, feeling their angry energies spreading throughout the convent.

Two weeks later Maurice announced that Father Dweyer insisted I be returned to his parish. "I'm against it. You haven't grown spiritually," she said through tight, dry lips.

As summer turned into fall, our busy school year teaching schedule began again. Judith was not transferred, although she continued to risk Maurice's discipline for our friendship. A placid and for the most part politely calm surface covered the uneasy truce with which Sister Maurice exercised her authority.

Soon it was spring again. It had been almost a year since my mother's visit. Just before Ash Wednesday, the beginning of the penance of Lent, I received a letter from my sister. She was deeply worried. "Mother hasn't been well lately. She's scheduled to go into the hospital in a couple of weeks for tests—something about her kidney. I'll keep you posted. You know how she is. Keeps all her problems to herself.

Guess what? I'm going to have a baby! My husband is delirious."

Eileen a mother? I felt terribly far from her. I hadn't shared the joy of her wedding. There would be another absence at the birth of her firstborn. In that moment I felt lonely and terribly sorry for myself. Six weeks would pass before I'd hear anything about my mother's condition. We weren't permitted to read our mail during Lent, a penance imposed on us by our Order, except for Superiors, who read all the mail.

When I found Maurice, she was washing linens in the basement. She didn't look up when I spoke to her.

"I'm worried about my mother's health," I said with painful effort to control my panic. "I need you to tell me if my mother's condition gets worse. I mean if she . . . may I just phone her now? Find out what's really happening? I'm sure it would cheer her and I wouldn't worry so. Six weeks is too long . . ."

Maurice never looked at me. "I'll let you know if anything serious develops, certainly. But this phone call is unwarranted. Really now, Roseann!" For an instant my passion to push Maurice's head under the soapy water sorely tempted me. She waved me away and I hurried upstairs, striking my breast in the familiar gesture of penance. *Mea culpa.* What was happening to my obedience, to my submission, to my willingness to joyfully embrace self-sacrifice?

Lenten fasting was never as difficult as not receiving my mail. Even our daily Rule of Silence, which banished all unnecessary conversation, was bearable when I could hear from home. When Mother Edmond's Lenten letter arrived, her message offered little consolation: "Unless we die to ourselves, we cannot hope to rise with Jesus on the glorious feast of the Resurrection." She added, "I will be visiting your convent in May and look forward to this time, when we will share our spiritual union."

I looked at the peaceful faces of the other Sisters, who seemingly had received this news with joyful hearts. Judith smiled at me kindly as Maurice posted Edmond's letter on the bulletin board. I couldn't help but wonder if Mother Edmond would find me as spiritually impoverished as my Superior found me to be.

After Easter Mass, I rushed to the community room to gather my mail, hungry for news from home. "Dear Elizabeth, Mother was taken to the hospital for a series of tests . . ."

The next letter read: "Mother underwent emergency surgery for a tumor near her kidney. Her heart stopped on the operating table. Phone, please . . ."

Still another letter read: "I have phoned Sister Maurice asking for you to come home. Mother has been terribly ill. Why haven't you responded?"

I slumped in my chair. My God! Mother's heart stopped? Maurice didn't tell me. But she had promised. Jesus! I couldn't think straight. Grabbing my mail, I tore through the convent, shouting, "Where's Maurice?"

The Sisters looked at me, bewildered.

"In the food cellar," one said.

"What's wrong?" Judith tried to stop me. "Calm down!"

I rushed past her. Maurice was crouched on the floor sorting out canned foods for the feast day dinner.

"You . . . you promised you'd tell me if anything serious happened to my mother."

"Roseann, stop screaming."

"Don't tell me to stop anything. Why didn't you tell me? Why?" I waved my letters wildly in her face. "My mother . . . oh, dear God, was dying. You knew it! I should have been with her. Dammit, why?"

Maurice stood, and affected a stance of smug tolerance. "Because your mother was recovering. Your sister, I felt, exaggerated the situation."

"Exaggerated? How in God's name dare you say such a thing? Woman, where is your mind? My mother will never forgive me. She won't understand, and her visit was cold enough . . . now this . . . my God!"

"Better get a hold on yourself, Sister Roseann. Visit the chapel. Ask for that control. I said it was my prudent judgment. Now leave me. Go to the chapel."

"Not until I phone my mother. Right now!" I moved closer to Maurice. "I've given my life to the Church, and what do I give my family, my sick mother, but pain! Pain!"

Maurice faced me coldly. "Your religious community is your family. Jesus is your family. Not get out of my sight and take your childish behavior with you!"

Backing from her, I turned and took three flights of stairs in seconds, slamming my bedroom door shut. I grabbed the statue of St. Joseph and bashed it against the sink. Reaching for the chair, I began beating it against the wall, screaming at the top of my lungs. "I hate the bitch! I hate her!"

Judith rushed into my room. "Stop it. Stop it, Roseann."

I fell against the wall, slipping to the floor, pounding my fist helplessly against the leg of my bed, sobbing while Judith spoke words I didn't hear. How could I have let Maurice do this to me? I didn't remember ever having felt such anger and hatred. What was happening to my vow of obedience? Under Maurice's jealously guarded authority I was learning disobedience, not obedience.

Judith stayed with me most of the day, but Maurice never came near us. "When Mother Edmond makes her visit, Roseann, ask for a transfer."

"But, Judith, I'm not a quitter."

"It's a matter of saving your soul, your heart, Roseann. That's not running; it's God-given survival."

"What will Mother Edmond think of me?"

"Does it matter so much what she thinks? You will have to survive many Superiors. You are young; they are not."

I wanted to confess and be cleansed of the hate I felt for Maurice, the guilt, the anger. I was sadly beginning to realize that my love for Jesus wasn't stronger than my weaknesses.

It was the following day when I realized I hadn't looked at one particular card from our old family friend Father Hart among my Easter mail. "Will be in New York at Fordham University with my law students for a debate tournament. Looking forward to visiting with you Easter Wednesday. It's been a long time . . ."

I smiled to myself. Father Hart would know about my mother's condition. It was an unexpected favor from Our Lord, despite my sinfulness. In the following days, I avoided Maurice as much as possible. I begged God to forgive me for hating her, but I continued to torment myself by questioning her authority. How could a woman like her manifest the will of God? *She* had sinned, not I.

Wednesday, Father Hart waited for me in the parlor. The last time I had seen him was when I was fifteen. As soon as he saw me, he threw out his thick teddy bear arms and hugged me warmly to his protruding middle, patting my head affectionately.

"You're a shade different from the last time, wearing shorts and running shoes for some . . ."

"Track competition."

"Ah, yes." His laugh lightened my heart. From out of his coat he pulled a huge box of chocolates. "Have a few bits before your Sisters devour the whole thing."

"But I'm not supposed to."

"I give you permission." He tore open the box, helping himself generously. The living room table was cheerfully decorated with spring lilies of the valley. Judith served him lunch and exited quickly. "And what do you think, Roseann, of our new Pope John XXIII?"

"I don't know too much about him." My lack of knowledge was a point of embarrassment. Mother Edmond continued to keep both secular and Catholic newspapers from us.

"Well," he said, "I have a feeling—just a feeling, mind you—that this Pontiff will shake the formidable rock of St. Peter." And he dove into his food hungrily. "Delicious," he said, disposing of the last bite.

"How is religious life treating you?" I could feel his keen eyes search for the truth he was accustomed to getting.

"I love my life, my missionary work, but probably I'll never get used to some things."

"Only some things, Roseann?"

"Well, being away from my family, my mother. Do you know how she is?" The poison of what had transpired broke open, my voice shook miserably, and I wasn't proud of how I felt.

Father Hart shook his napkin over his plate. "Saw your mother every day in the hospital. Why didn't you visit her or at least call, Roseann?"

Father Hart listened, gently kicking the table leg with the tip of his shoe. "So that's the story. Ask your good Superior to come in, please. I would like to, shall we say, share my thoughts with her." Tiny red veins were popping out on his face, making it nearly as red as his hair.

I dreaded finding Maurice, who was assisting Judith in the kitchen. She followed me cheerfully into the parlor.

"Have you enjoyed your lunch?" she asked with the particular charm she reserved for the clergy.

"Most enjoyable. Excellent decor." He gestured Maurice to sit opposite him. I fingered my rosary beads nervously as Father Hart's voice became hard and angry.

"I've known Roseann and her mother for years," he said, holding Maurice's gaze with his own. "You knew how critically ill—near death—her mother was?"

Maurice nodded and arched her back.

"What is your explanation for not telling Roseann of her mother's condition?" he demanded. The red hairs of his eyebrows stood out.

Sister Maurice pushed her chair back and scowled at me. "It was my judgment that the situation was under control. Lent is the time for penance. Roseann knows that. We aren't permitted home visits, phone calls . . . the Holy Rule," she said stiffly.

I watched the pupils of Father Hart's eyes contract. "My

good Superior, love of family supersedes this Holy Rule of yours. Always! I am reminded of the rule of St. Benedict. It is one of *moderation,* my dear Sister Maurice, not just a diet of penance. St. Benedict knew that too much fasting and discipline resulted in lethargy, the lack of Godliness that leads to sickness. Charity begins in our hearts, in the care we give to the ones we love. Any holy rule that negates this is not holy, Sister. It is a cursed enigma, an insult to the love of God to which we give our lives." He stood up, towering over her as he continued, "Do you understand what I am trying to tell you, Sister Superior?"

She nodded silently, digging her heels into the floor.

"Now, Sister," he said, pointing, "you see the phone over there?"

She nodded again.

"Bring it here, because Roseann is going to make a long distance call to her mother. She will talk as long as she pleases."

Maurice set the phone on the table, her eyes darting between me and the instrument of my defiance.

Father Hart's voice was gruff. "You had better leave before I begin to regret what else I might say to you."

Her face turned from an angry flush to the color of paste as she left the parlor.

I held the phone as if it were a sacred chalice. My thoughts were racing. What could I say? Hart smiled reassuringly, dipping once more into the candy box.

When I heard the familiar voice of my mother, my voice broke, in spite of my desire to control myself for her sake. "Mother . . . Mother."

"Honey, it's all right. I don't blame you. It's all right."

We talked for a long time. "Mother, I pray for you every day. You're never far from my thoughts, and if I could, I'd be home nursing you." With those words, I wept.

For the first time in days I felt better, cleansed and forgiven. Father Hart smiled. "Remember this, Roseann. Love comes before all else, and charity gives us the permission to practice it."

The words and way he rocked back and forth in his chair reminded me of Father Barrett, and I couldn't resist the temptation to ask, "Have you heard of a Father Barrett?" I was holding my breath.

"And who hasn't?" He laughed. "I'll probably see him in Georgetown this week. That's generally where he stays when he isn't flying around the country, no doubt seducing nuns with the love of Jesus." He winked broadly.

For the next few minutes I shared my memories of the Retreat of the Smiling Faces.

"Wonderful man! Wonderful man!" Father Hart kept saying, even as he scribbled Father Barrett's address on a scrap of paper. "Drop him a line," he said. "I'm sure he'd love to hear from you. The man has an ego, after all, and you're a pretty one. In the service of God, of course." He laughed. I had waited for this for three years; certainly the divine providence of this favor was a smile from Jesus.

Father Hart glanced at his watch. "If you don't get me to the bus fast, I'll be here hours longer. That will break your Superior's heart." He grinned widely, satisfied. I, too, was grinning smugly, struck by the irony of Sister Maurice trying to teach me obedience to her authority and succeeding instead in teaching me to subvert it.

❦ 8 ❦

Mother Edmond was expected to arrive at the end of the week. We scoured every square inch of our convent as if it were the body of a leper. Father Dweyer sent Mario, his own parish gardener, to trim the hedges and plant pansies, sweet williams, and marigolds for the occasion. As I drove up the convent driveway, a tall dark young man was working beside Mario, stripped to his waist, exposing strong, hard shoulders. I stopped to watch them work. "My nephew," shouted Mario pleasantly. The young man turned. There was something about his sensual mouth, his dark Italian eyes, and the smooth olive-amber texture of his skin that made me tremble.

I could feel his eyes follow me as I drove into the garage. I heard footsteps behind the car. Without looking at me, he dropped a small bouquet of pansies through the window onto my lap, the petals spreading over my habit skirt. I did not want to think about how he made me feel, but I could not seem to help it.

Thursday, Mother Edmond arrived and took her seat at the head of the table. There was nothing Sister Maurice did not think of to please the Mother General. Our cooks, Sisters Judith and Gerald, served the meals and the Sisters' artificially happy behavior created a strained, unreal atmosphere. Mother Edmond visited all the pastors we worked for, appraising our work and listening to their complaints, if they dared make any.

I was the last Sister to have a private visit with Mother Edmond before she returned to the Motherhouse. The sunlight through the parlor window caught her veil, and in spite of her apparent fatigue, she looked radiant. She gestured for me to sit beside her. I was silent. I dared not complain of Sister Maurice, not to a woman such as Mother Edmond, whose religious ideals surely were formed in heaven.

"Roseann, you must keep your heart steadfast and detached from all human comfort, from all *particular* friendships, and from wanting the satisfaction of results from your work." As she spoke, I knew Sister Maurice had primed her. I avoided her gaze until our conference ended.

"Remember me in your prayers?" I asked, as was the custom at the end of any conference.

"I have always done that, Sister Roseann," she said with her familiar half smile.

I was exhausted from Mother Edmond's visit, from the demands of protocol. I wondered if Judith had spoken her mind to Mother Edmond and if any of the other senior Sisters had complained about Sister Maurice. But I found my thoughts drifting more to the young gardener, to his sensual smile. Men . . . boys . . . if only they'd disappear from my mind. But they returned relentlessly to haunt me, particularly when I was exhausted. The temptation to drag my twisted nightgown between my legs grew. "Lord, you are my strength," I prayed. "In your presence the devil has no power."

Not long after Mother Edmond had left us, Sister Maurice read the anxiously awaited letter listing the Sisters to be transferred. My name was at the top of the list. Even though I might have expected it, still the news stunned me. Maurice continued to speak in a monotone. "I don't want any of you mentioning your transfers to your pupils or to the priests.

This is my responsibility after you've left." She glanced in my direction, and all the Sisters turned to stare at me. "Remember, this is our community custom. When we practice the spirit of detachment, it will help us live only for Jesus."

I fled to the chapel, depressed. No good-byes, uprooted from everyone I had grown to love. I'd be transferred before I could whisper farewell to Father Dweyer, to the families, the children I'd worked with. Would they ever know how much I loved them?

This was how Sister Maurice had pulled me away from Harlem, away from my unfinished work with Manuel. The pain of that memory still cut deeply into my being. Verdine had seen it as a test of my vow of obedience. It seemed that everyone but me accepted obedience to a Superior as the equivalent of obedience to God. Why must I be the one to ask how a loving God could will such cold unfeeling endings? In Harlem I had left Manuel; here I would be leaving Jerome, another troubled young man.

Jerome's family had been long-time residents and seemingly tireless participants in parish activities. The nuns in our convent had known him since he was a child. They had helped prepare him for his First Communion and Confirmation; they had seen him become an altar boy, had watched his determination to become a priest grow, nurtured by his mentor, Father Dweyer.

When I first met him, he was a senior in high school, as I would have been had I not entered the convent. He was a tall, slender young man, almost delicate-looking, with a fervent conviction of the rightness of his vocation to the priesthood. His family were encouraging him to go to college for a few years, particularly his older sister, Jean, who had attended Julliard School of Music before coming back to marry and have a family and later to become the parish music director. But Jerome was determined and looked on me as an ally in this, since my family had let me go even before high school graduation. He won out and entered the seminary the year we were both eighteen.

After that first year, he came home for a six-week vacation every summer. Although he was expected to work in the parish and to live in the rectory with the priests, he still had ample opportunities to visit with his family. Each year I looked forward to his coming; on hot summer afternoons we would sit in the cool dimness at the back of the church and talk. Often after choir practice, Jean would join us there.

The ban on unnecessary conversation and the Rules of Silence among the nuns were not so rigidly enforced for conversations between the nuns and priests and between the nuns and parishioners, particularly if the priests or parishioners initiated the conversations. I suppose because of that, and because Jerome was such a favorite of everyone, I was not reprimanded when we would meet and talk at the parish.

He would talk of his studies. How envious I was of the education he was receiving! He had one more year in the seminary before his ordination into the priesthood. But this last summer he was different somehow, sometimes preoccupied and restless, sometimes talking excitedly about the kind of priest he would be. His physical changes were as marked as his moods. He had grown noticeably thinner, almost gaunt; his usually fair skin at times looked gray.

On the Sunday of his second week at home, he attended the same High Mass as the nuns. After the Sisters had received Holy Communion, Jerome approached the altar rail, where suddenly his hand knotted in a tight fist. With uncanny speed, he lashed out and smashed Father Dweyer in the face, sending him sprawling to the sanctuary floor. The contents of the ciborium scattered over the dark red carpet.

For a few seconds Jerome stared at the stunned priest in bewilderment, then he slumped forward over the altar rail. Jean rushed from the organ, grabbed his arm, and led him stumbling blindly from the church. He was admitted to

Rosecrest, the most prestigious recovery hospital in the diocese, that afternoon.

Hours later, Jean and I walked down Rosecrest's thick blue carpeted corridor to a private room to see her brother.

"I sign you both with the sign of the cross," he said solemnly as we entered. "I give you the power to forgive sin, the power to heal." In the same hushed tone of voice he continued, "You damn son of a bitches . . . lewd despicable sinners!" He started to gesture wildly. "Get behind me! Get behind me, Satan!" He half sat up in his bed, saliva dripping from the corners of his mouth. We left badly shaken.

On the way out Jean spoke briefly to the head psychiatrist, Dr. Wheeler, a tall middle-aged man. I listened, feeling a deep sense of sadness for Jerome.

"He's fasted past his body's endurance," Dr. Wheeler offered gently at first, then, warming to his pet subject of ecclesiastical patients, he added, "His nerves are frayed. Too much study, too much discipline, I think."

"Can he return to the seminary?" Jean asked, her voice unsteady.

"Well, in my opinion, your brother should never have been accepted to the seminary in the first place. He'll recover with rest and treatment, but if he returns to the doctrine, I'm sorely afraid that he'll relapse."

In three weeks Jerome was seemingly put together, a rather patchy mental Humpty Dumpty. He had gained some weight, filling out his six-foot frame handsomely. His eyes were bright and lively and they followed the young nurses.

The seminary accepted him back, but on a trial basis. He had been back a month when Jean called me at the convent. "Jerome is doing well," she said. "Dr. Wheeler must have just been overcautious." Her voice was somewhat prim. At the time I felt she had been ashamed of her brother's breakdown. "Hope to see you soon," she added. "And you must come to rehearsal; we're preparing the Charpentier 'Te

Deum.'" She hung up. In spite of her reassurance, a doubt of my own hung in clamorous silence.

Weeks later Jean sought me in the convent parlor, her face blotchy, mascara smeared under her eyes. "They've taken Jerome to the hospital in a straitjacket. Four seminarians had to restrain him." What little comfort I could share with Jean was feeble at best. By comparison, my troubles were insignificant, I told myself.

Jerome grew steadily worse and was finally transferred to the state hospital, where he took up a tiny life, living in a tiny, padded solitary cell.

Jean usually called me after her hospital visits with Jerome. "His condition remains the same. He says Mass constantly in his cell, but he can't associate with the other patients." She hesitated. "I told Father Dweyer I thought he was possessed. It's possible, you know."

"My God, Jean . . ."

"I don't know why . . ." She sobbed. "Father Dweyer visited Jerome yesterday," she finally said. "He told me that I have to face the fact Jerome has suffered a psychotic episode, that trying to make myself think he's possessed is . . . is . . . but it hurts so much. He doesn't even know me."

In another call she told me about his case psychiatrist, Dr. Ortiz, and how, in an effort to establish some kind of communication with Jerome, the doctor had contrived to have the back wall of Jerome's cell painted to resemble the main altar of a Catholic church. "I told Dr. Ortiz about you," Jean added, "that you were Jerome's friend, that he had probably confided in you more than anyone. The doctor thinks it might help if you come with me on my next visit."

Sister Maurice very reluctantly granted permission for the visit. I felt that she, like too many others in the parish, would have preferred to ignore the whole incident, hoping that by pretending it never happened, it would somehow go away.

Jean and I watched as two husky psychiatric technicians led Jerome back to his room and stripped him of his straitjacket, running from his clawing hands. He tore off his clothes and yelled obscenities. He began to crawl on all fours, crying, pleading for someone to open his cage door, saliva dripping from his mouth. I couldn't stand to look at him any longer. We moved out of his line of sight as he began to creep toward the painted wall. He reached out tentatively to pat it with childlike reverence. Then he began to cry, not wild hysterical sobs, but a deep, quiet grieving that sounded to me as sane as any sorrowing human can sound. He caressed the painted altar, the large crucifix; his raging stopped and only the sound of deep spasms crossed the room.

Jerome stood tall, garbed in a kind of priestly dignity despite his utter nakedness. He gently picked up a Bible, opened it, and began to read quietly to himself as he paced the small room. We watched as he folded his body tightly on the floor pad against the painted altar wall and fell asleep. I wiped my eyes with the sleeve of my habit, unable to speak. Jean and I left the hospital in silence.

It was hours later that I realized I had seen a man's naked body for the first time. The fading face of Father Barrett returned, the longing looks of the boys I taught, the light-hearted smile of Father Johnson, the handsome face of Father Dweyer, and even the forbidden pleasure of the night before my final vows. But for Jerome, I felt only the pain of his suffering.

Jerome had not recognized me and probably would not recognize me if I were to see him again. But would Jean really understand why I didn't say good-bye, why I couldn't go with her to visit him the next time?

I begged God to have mercy on Jerome, who wanted in life only to serve Jesus. It broke my heart to see the cost. Judith had told me often, "You must let it all go or you'll lose your own way." I want to live, I want to love, I cried out silently to my invisible Spouse Jesus in the tabernacle.

My plain black suitcase creased the middle of my white bed. I packed six pairs of long white cotton underwear, one black habit, two black and white veils, and black cotton stockings. Finally, I was left with only my deep red scarf, the edges frayed now and beginning to fade. It was a gay woolen lover in disguise, a somehow shocking contrast to the black and white world around me.

I lifted the red scarf to my lips and kissed it as tenderly as I would have my dearest friend. "Keep my scarf with you, Elizabeth. Don't part with it ever, promise me," Eileen had insisted. She had worn it every time we ran in competition, reminding us of the flaming Olympic torch we had once dreamed of carrying. I folded the scarf carefully, putting it in the deepest corner of my suitcase.

Mother Edmond had admonished me to "give up every attachment, personal and material. It will make you an empty vessel to be filled with the grace of your Spouse Jesus." I slid a small pocket mirror beside the scarf. I am so aware, Mother Edmond, that I disobey you in this, but I will not part with my scarf. Never.

Sister Judith called softly from the hall. Even as I was opening the door, she kissed me lightly on my forehead and pressed a small envelope into my hands. She was gone before I could touch her. Judith! She didn't look back, merely disappeared down the stairs. I gave myself permission to open the envelope only as I left the convent for the waiting car.

"Oh, the comfort, the inexpressible comfort, of feeling safe with a person, having neither to weigh thoughts nor measure moods, but express them just as they are, chaff and grain together, certain that a faithful hand will take and shift them, keep what is worth keeping and, with the breath of kindness, blow the rest away."

"Spare me, Lord," I prayed, "from the likes of another Sister Maurice. Send me someone kind and loving as Judith." It was a desperate plea for a small cup of happiness, which I knew was not the embrace of Christ's Cross, to test my weak faith and my shallow obedience.

ST. MICHAEL'S CONVENT
Albany, New York

⚜ 9 ⚜

St. Michael's Convent in Albany was impressive, with its oak parquet floors and windows penetrating the first story from wainscot to the embossed ceilings overhead. Mother Edmond had been the reigning Superior at St. Michael's for years. Even Verdine had flourished here. I was beginning this assignment with a sense of anticipation I had not felt in a long time.

I was to share a second-floor dormitory room with Sisters Janice and Mariann. Six of us shared a small bathroom on the third floor. I would miss my private attic room at Ronston, but changes would keep me humble, I reminded myself, lest I begin to revel in material comforts.

Sister Janice was about ten years older than I and had been at St. Michael's for several years. She was bright and quick and self-confident. She often wore the mocking expression of someone greatly enjoying a private joke. Sister Mariann was a year younger than I and, like me, was newly arrived at St. Michael's. In contrast to Sister Janice, Sister Mariann was slow and methodical. Large wire-rim glasses dominated her plain face.

That first afternoon after spiritual reading, our Superior, Sister Martha, gathered all of the Sisters together. "I wish to welcome Sisters Mariann and Roseann to our Albany mission." I glanced around the room and the Sisters were smiling slightly. "I'm pleased to announce that Roseann has been appointed my Assistant Superior." She paused. "I will miss Sister Lisa, but Mother Edmond made an excellent choice in appointing her Superior of our New Haven convent." Sister Martha lifted her head higher. "Lisa, as my assistant, was the kind of person I could depend on. She paid attention to detail. She is a perfect example of our Holy Rule of Silence." Sister Martha shot me a cold look, making her point clear.

By becoming the Assistant Superior, I was one step away from the coveted status of Superiorship. It was the recognition of spiritual achievement, the mark of Mother Edmond's approval. I wanted this title as much as sainthood and I vowed to prove myself worthy of Mother Edmond's surprising trust in me. After Sister Martha's opening remarks, I wondered what it would cost.

Sister Janice scanned the bulletin board later and her name was next to Cathedral parish, given to Sisters with the most diverse experience in social work. Cathedral abided uneasily in the heart of Albany's ghetto, like some lush, thorned rose surrounded by the parched flowers of the depressed poor.

My name was next to St. George's parish, where Bishop Smithsonia was pastor. It shocked me. My years of experience in Ronston had given me some exposure to the higher level of powerful men in the Church. But would I be equal to working for a Bishop?

That first night in Albany was a fitful one. The wire coils of my simple bed protested under the shifting weight of restless sleep. I felt a terrible lump of loneliness for Sister Judith, for faces of familiar children, for Father Johnson. Sister Martha's harsh expectations troubled me. She didn't work in the parishes, as did most of our Superiors. Her prime occupation was spiritual director to *her* Sisters, assigned by herself to herself, "in keeping with the standards of Mother Edmond, of course," she insisted. I remembered the coldness of her stare. Cold was an apt word for her. She seemed so in every way. In spite of her ruddy skin and squarely built frame, she frequently wore a sweater over her habit, even in the summer, when most of us were sweltering under our heavy black woolen robes. She hovered over us like a screech owl, making sure our parish work matched her own standards of perfection.

"You're expected to turn in a hundred census cards and twenty case cards twice a month," she told me flatly as I prepared to work in the parish.

"But I haven't done such work in years."

She looked up from the neat piles of cards on her desk. "I said it's expected. You are a working member of the Bishop's staff, my dear lazy Roseann."

"Whose expectations are they? The Bishop's?"

"Mine. Lisa managed without complaint. Certainly you can." She smiled tightly and my stomach tightened. "We visit Bishop Smithsonia Friday."

"Sister Martha, I want to make something clear from the start."

"Really now, your wants are not the issue, Roseann."

"But I feel they are important. I am not your former assistant Lisa. I don't intend to be her. I won't compete with her, and I pray that I be given the freedom not to be compared to her."

Martha said nothing, only dismissed me with a wave of her hand.

Friday morning I knelt before the gold-veiled tabernacle in the center of the rich walnut altar of the convent chapel. "Lord, cast from my heart all doubt and bless my new mission, my parish." I strained to add Martha's name to my prayer.

Sister Martha and I walked the four blocks to St. George's in strained, reinforced silence. Her step was firm and her eyes were cast down to the pavement. How curious, I thought, that she looks down when I felt it was all up ahead of us.

The rectory, all of Italian marble, was as elegant as the church itself. Bishop Smithsonia offered his hand to me. I knelt and kissed his ring, a symbol of his office, in the traditional greeting given a Bishop. When I looked at him I felt a powerful presence emanating from his person. Quietly, I watched the Bishop ponder each case and assign it to one of his four assistants—four because, after all, he was the Bishop.

"You'll like St. George's, Sister Roseann," the Bishop said.

I was unwilling to dampen any expectations this beaming man had for me. "I know I will. But I have a small doubt that my skills might not be equal to the intellectual needs of your parish."

Sister Martha spoke at once. "Your Excellency, Sister Roseann has education on her mind these days, something I feel the changing Church has aroused."

He ran his thin finger down his chin thoughtfully. "Education is in the experience. I am pleased you have brought me an inquiring mind. Sister Roseann, I'm sure, will add diligence to my staff."

In the first months at St. George's I was elated at the chance to visit families outside the convent's limiting confines, polishing my counseling skills. However, the apathy of the rich and their indifference to their spiritual welfare was something I had not quite encountered with the poor of Harlem or in Ronston. Problems of rich people were too many divorces, secret love affairs, and boring social lives. I found myself envying Sister Janice's work with the poor. At least they were unpretentious.

It didn't take me long to learn that all of Sister Martha's spare time was spent in white-gloving the Sister's house work. "She's a neurotic pick," Janice whispered during one silence time.

"I believe she doesn't have enough *real* work to do," I

said. Janice laughed. Though I watched our Superior worry each Sister, she relished castigating Janice, whose dedication to her work seemed to anger Martha.

That evening when I passed Martha's office Janice was thrusting her files fiercely onto Martha's desk. "I'm taking these families to the welfare office Monday. I can't leave them starving. They are desperate. No one wants to help them and—"

"Janice, your mission is to care for their spiritual needs, nothing more and nothing less! That's what the pastor wants, and his wishes will be obeyed."

"But that's not what he told me," Janice insisted.

Martha's voice was ice. "Do as I say!"

Janice left the office. "Ignorant, arrogant, insensitive bitch!" she muttered as she tore past me, nearly knocking me down. She would take loving care of God's work in her parish in her own way. She was tough, a veteran nun with too much experience to be bullied by anyone—least of all Martha. How many years would it take me to grow a hide like hers, to survive, as Judith had warned me I must learn to do.

When I handed my parish clerical work to Sister Martha, she was still fuming and dove into it, tearing it apart as she must have wished she could have done with Janice. "You have no mind for detail, Roseann," and she red-clipped most of my cards. "My assistant will excel, even at simple parish work," she barked.

I was forced to listen, waiting for the moment I'd be free of her anger.

It was the feast of St. Teresa, the patron of our Mother Foundress, and Janice had prepared a splendid roast lamb dinner. I couldn't help but marvel how this nun seemed to do everything well, making Sister Martha's hostility more pointed. It was after supper that Sister Martha announced, "Mother Edmond has assigned Sister Ruth of Chicago to lead us in a week of theology classes."

I remembered Sister Ruth. She'd been sent to Catholic

University this last summer to take classes. The impact of Pope John XXIII could no longer be ignored, not even by Mother Edmond. It was no secret that Sister Ruth was being mentored by her Superior, Sister Denise. She might easily be appointed Superior in the summer.

"Ruth will be a revitalizing change," Janice said as we washed dishes together in the kitchen. Sister Martha was out of hearing, and we were ignoring the ban on unnecessary conversation.

I speculated, "I wonder why I wasn't chosen to take those courses instead of Ruth." It was a petty remark, but I couldn't help myself.

"Come on, Roseann. You know as well as I do. Religious life is no different from politics in the world."

"Where does God's will fit in?" By now I was feeling defensive. Politics felt ugly, unclean. The very idea that our fates depended on how our Superiors felt about us, regardless, of our spiritual or natural abilities, sickened me.

Janice took a moment before answering. "The will of God enters through our faith and that takes a lot of faith."

The snow had begun to fall when Sister Ruth arrived from Chicago. She was short at d plump, but she handled herself with a natural dignity that made her seem taller than she was. Although she was not pretty, her pleasant and attentive expression kept her from being plain. Sister Ruth spoke with authority and confidence, as if she could easily be a Mother General. She had a clarity of vision that Mother Edmond could never allow herself. "Change is necessary for growth," Ruth offered. "The only thing that doesn't change is light. We must seek light to open our minds to the teachings of Pope John XXIII and his Vatican Councils, to the spirit of love and to the good will of the Gospels." Martha nodded her head during the class. Janice took copious notes, and I noticed that the other Sisters watched every move Ruth made.

Even though I did not want to admit it to myself, I was terribly envious of Ruth. I longed to go to Catholic University, to stand where she now stood. The guilt from my envy led me to discipline myself, to pray harder for humility. Still, my thirst for approval from my Superiors, from Mother Edmond, and for the power to be in control never left me.

For five days Ruth opened gaping windows of hope through her seminars. I felt then like some half-starved dog gnawing at bones of knowledge, and I grew insatiably curious for information about the forbidden world. When a parish woman offered me her newspaper, I took it. Later, when I was hiding it in my community room drawer, I felt a hand on my shoulder. "Taking liberties, Roseann?" Martha pulled it out of my hands and returned to her office, where she snapped the door firmly closed.

After our final theology class, I approached Ruth, hating to see her leave. She was taking the comfort of her knowledge away from us. "I want so much to learn," I said, hating myself for indulging in ambitions denied me. She smiled kindly and in that moment I wanted to be her friend.

"Keep praying, dreaming, Roseann," she offered. "My circumstances weren't much different from yours a year ago. Trust in the Heart of Jesus."

I needed to hear this, to hold on to some thin thread of reassurance.

❧ 10 ❧

I drove into St. George's parish, delighted to have the car at my disposal. Driving had become a wonderful pleasure. My last call was to a one-story brick house on Elm Street.

A pleasant, smiling woman welcomed me into the living room. "I don't live here, actually. Just spending a few weeks with my son. He's divorced." She confided that he didn't have much respect for the Church's doctrine.

While she was busy whispering embarrassing family secrets, I heard a door open and close. Then a dark-haired young giant entered, kissed his mother lightly on the cheek, and sat down on the couch opposite me. He closed his eyes wearily. "My name is Jonathan," he said, his eyes still closed. "What's yours?"

"I am called Sister Roseann within the confines of the Church."

He began laughing and I found myself swept up in the rolling sound he made. "Confines? Let's see. How much would the Church measure? Who does the contracting? Nah . . . don't take me seriously . . . just a little tired. Maybe Mom wants to get me a brew." There was an animal familiarity about the manner in which he had entered and allowed his presence simply to permeate everything. The man had no self-consciousness. I admired this while wishing he were not so close.

"How about a beer, Sister? You allowed to drink on duty?"

"Now, now, Jonathan, we know how you feel about the Church, but we must be polite," his mother said.

The hall clock chimed and I used this as an excuse to announce that I was late for convent prayer.

"I hope you will return soon, Sister," Mrs. Randall said quietly.

"I'll come back tomorrow."

Jonathan's eyes followed me to the door. It would take time to work with a man as spiritually hardened as Jonathan, I thought. Repeated home visits could inspire a spiritual victory, a victory that would please Our Lord, Bishop Smithsonia, and the Sisters.

For the rest of the day Jonathan's deep mellow voice echoed in my head. The intensity of his eyes haunted me. I told myself, not only the poor and the downtrodden must be saved, but beautiful people as well.

When I approached the house the next day, I firmly resolved to enter only if Jonathan's mother was home.

Mrs. Randall greeted me warmly. "I'm delighted you returned, Sister Roberta."

"Roseann," I corrected.

"Oh yes, Roseann it is. Forgive me. Nun names are so confusing." She waved me to the couch. I could hear sounds coming from a back room, and my body stiffened as Jonathan entered.

His mother rose quickly. "I'm so scatterbrained, Jonnie. I almost forgot my dental appointment. If I keep this up, I'll be wearing dentures."

I rose as she did, almost reached out to clutch her and keep her there. "If I'd known you wouldn't be here, I could have made another appointment."

"Don't worry, Sister, we can talk Church talk some other

day. My son here needs more conversion than I do. He'll tell you, no doubt, about Catholic school." She laughed lightly.

Jonathan kicked absently at the edge of the throw-rug. "How the nuns beat on my knuckles. Hell, who'd forget that? Think you'll have a hard time making a convert out of me, Sister. But if you have something more interesting in mind, maybe we can make a little deal. Know what I mean?"

"Now, Jonnie, the good nun has been sent by the Church. Stop baiting her, and show her the good grace of respect," she added. "Be good."

I watched her leave, knowing I should be following her. I couldn't bring myself to move.

"Do you know of a Sister Mauritius? She was my eighth-grade teacher."

"No. I didn't know you'd had any Catholic school education until your mother mentioned it."

"Hated it, actually. My mother's the religious fanatic in the family. But this nun, the only one I really liked. You remind me somehow of her. I can't get over it." I laughed at his candor, and Jonathan leaned back against his chair, stretching his legs out between us. "Too bad you didn't meet me *before* you became a nun."

Uneasy sensations worked down my spine. We had talked too long already about things that had nothing to do with the fact that he refused to practice the faith of his birth. I rose to leave with dragging reluctance.

"I want you to come back," he said, "please come back." And he took my hand for a moment, frightening me.

"Tell your mother I'll be back tomorrow."

That evening I pulled the thick drapes close around my bed and invited in the thought of Jonathan, his work-hardened hands, his full mouth. Visit him one more time?

The following morning Jonathan answered the door. "You just missed Mother." His shirt was unbuttoned. "Come in, please."

We had a rule: Never enter a house where the man is

alone. I understood its wisdom and yet I followed him into the living room, grateful for the sofa that gave relief to my wobbly knees.

Heat poured off my body when he sat down next to me. Jonathan's voice floated heavy and distant through my self-absorbed vision. "What do you do in the convent all day?" He laughed. "Full of secrets, I suppose."

"Not what you think." I felt awkward. "Each day begins with prayer. In fact our entire schedule offers us opportunities for service, as a community of nuns and in our parishes."

He talked about his work as a contractor and asked me more about my life. To my surprise, before long I was resting easily on the couch, laughing and telling him about Ruth's seminar and my hopes.

Jonathan grew intent as he listened and I felt I was the center of his attention. He sprawled out, his legs spread carelessly apart. As we talked I couldn't keep my eyes off the cloth tightening over the swelling curve between his legs. Hot prickles were covering my face and I turned my head away, still seeing his swelling groin in my mind's eye. I felt a panicked need to rise, to run away, and an equally mad desire to reach out and touch his thigh. My fingers moved restlessly in my lap.

"Sister?"

My face was burning. I looked at my watch. "I . . . I'm sorry, I'm running late. A bad habit lately, I'm afraid." I managed to stand, embarrassed by the feel of wet underclothes and the intense heat pulsing through my body. He followed me to the door.

"Wait." I stood there stony. I heard him gently beg, "Please turn around, just for a minute." I started to turn, not able to look at him.

"Please . . ." I said weakly, but I continued turning.

"You're too beautiful to be a nun. Don't you ever want to make love?"

I wanted to scream YES! In forbidden dreams, in my loneliness. I bit hard on my lip. All I had to do was turn back and open the door and I'd be free.

But even as Jonathan spoke he moved his body to imprison me against the closed door. He thrust his hardness up against the folds of my heavy woolen habit to home between my legs. A blinding thrill of sensation overwhelmed me, and I sagged against the door. With one arm he supported me and pulled me tightly against his chest. With a single swift movement his head bent to capture my mouth with his and his free hands pulled my face closer, then dropped to slide down the slope of my chest. His mouth explored mine, his tongue flicking the inner flesh of my lips with a tantalizing restraint that made me want to push my mouth hard against him, grab a handful of his dark hair.

Frantic at my own feelings, I flailed against him with arms that had lost their strength. His fingers quickly invaded my cape and I began to sag and nearly fell when he took his arm from around me.

I felt his hands on my hips pulling me in against him in slow, demanding rhythm. My whole body shook violently in an uncontrollable spasm, and I lost myself in a moment of pleasure such as I had never experienced. "Come, sweetness." He rubbed his groin tighter, harder, against me.

My head cleared as he pulled back my veil. The room seemed crystal bright and fragile in its sharp lines that were real beyond reality. I seemed to tower above Jonathan, who without ceasing his thrusting rhythm had pulled a little away and bent to rub his mouth and face against my exposed breast. I pushed him off with a power that amazed me. My left arm came alive as I grabbed the door knob behind me.

Jonathan seemed in shock. "You can't go." He reached for me as I twisted the knob, my control returning. "You'll be back for more." His breathing was labored. He moved partly through the doorway, then stopped abruptly. "You're a lot of woman. You don't even know it." I ran down the steps, but his voice followed me as I opened the car door. "You don't want this God stuff. You'll be back, Roseann."

Three blocks away, an overwhelming weakness nearly caused me to drive into another car. I steered into the curb, parked, dropped my head in my hands. What had possessed me to stay? I had felt the overwhelmingly intense pleasure of a man's play, the power of his body. How could I ever erase the memory? I tried to regain control of myself. He was wrong. He had to be wrong. But I knew it was my sin, not Jonathan's entirely.

By the time I returned to the convent, I was drowning in a sea of guilt and shame. I had to confess. It was selfish indulgence of the worst kind. During the night I heard the grandfather's clock chime on the hour, reminding me of the eternity I should spend in hell. Each toss in my cot recalled Jonathan's arms pressing me closer to the warmth of his body, shaking me with excitement. His memory consumed me with as much pleasure as it tormented me with the thought of hell.

My habit was drenched when I entered the confessional. "Father, I have sinned grievously against my vow of chastity."

My confessor coughed. "The circumstances, Sister? Perhaps they are not as serious as you imagine." It was a natural conclusion of any confessor, because nuns were known for their constant state of scrupulosity.

"I fear it is quite grievous, Father." I poured out the story and in the telling I wanted to be punished, hating myself because even in the memory Jonathan aroused me. "Will I get over this . . . wanting the pleasure?"

"Jesus is merciful." Father Ostoff's voice was surprisingly tender. "He permits our weakness to teach humility and compassion. But you must never see this man again."

"I won't. Ever, Father."

"And do you have close friends in whom you can confide?"

"Sister Judith, but she's in New Jersey. No, no one here."

He mumbled something I heard as "pity." "I'm here for

you as your confessor any time you need to unburden yourself. The weight of this cross will not be easy to carry, but Jesus never intended we carry our crosses alone."

"I fear my weakness, my desires."

"Learn then to live with them, one day at a time. It is God's way, Sister."

My body sagged heavily. "But Jonathan held me, he listened to me. I felt it even if it lasted only a moment. In our religious community the Sisters are forbidden to touch, to become friends. We live in a world of silence. I am starved for those things that make me sinful." With the sleeve of my habit, I wiped my cheeks.

"Religious life is the Way of the Cross, Sister. No one promised you different." Father Ostoff sucked in a breath.

"Will my penance, my imposed sacrifices, bring back the grace, the blessings, I had before I met this man?" I wanted to scream from the tightness of my bowels, from the icy feeling gripping me.

"Bless God and learn patience, Sister. For your penance, traverse the Stations of the Cross. Meditate deeply on the stations where Jesus fell, the fifth station with Simon of Cyrene. Our blessed Lord allowed Himself to be helped. Remember this. It might ease your suffering."

Despite his understanding, I experienced no peace. There wasn't a day when I didn't remember the heat of my desire or feel Jonathan's needs. My breasts felt especially tender. Like a punishing whip, my mind refused to allow me to forget anything. For weeks I spoke frequently with Father Ostoff, giving him the opportunity to practice the virtue of patience. "Time is the greatest healer of all," he offered simply.

Every time I prayed the Hail Mary—"*Pray for us sinners now and at the hour of our death*"—it was with keener understanding than I'd ever had. I was a sinner, weak and vulnerable. I remembered Manuel, the product, the victim, of Harlem's ghetto. By contrast, I had been given abundant graces as a Bride of Christ, and I had poisoned that faith and trust. In the nearly automatic gesture of contrition, I closed my right hand into a soft fist and gently and repeatedly struck the inside of my left breast. *Mea culpa.*

❦ 11 ❦

There were times of respite from the pain. One morning we were invited to attend Mass honoring the patron saint feast day at the novitiate of the Sisters of St. Joseph, whose training house was located just three doors from our convent. We seldom saw these nuns and their young novices because they were a thorn in Sister Martha's side. "They live too worldly in their religious life, indulge in many corrupting privileges of the world," she complained as we walked the short distance in the crisp morning air.

"I love these nuns," I said. In that moment I wanted to challenge her fear. "They gave me nothing but love as my teachers in grade school. They were my friends."

Sister Martha turned her face and clutched her ever-present sweater closer over her shoulders.

When the young Sisters came into their chapel, I saw the familiar faces of Sisters Joel and Daniel, whom I had first met at a catechetical workshop in New York. They smiled their greetings and gestured in small finger waggings.

Minutes after we'd returned to the convent, Joel was on the phone. "We'd like to visit with you. I can't believe we're only houses apart."

"Come now. Please!" For the first time in months, I felt

lighthearted. A short while later, when the two novices walked up our path, Martha saw them and her face darkened. "Who invited them?"

"I did."

"I want no socializing with these nuns. Their lives will upset our serenity."

I took her bait. "We are all religious, serving the same Lord, the same Church, and who are we to judge which is more holy?" We faced each other angrily; the novices were at our door.

"Make this the last time they visit our convent, Roseann. I'm warning you." She hurried out through the back parlor door.

Janice came out of the chapel and winked at me. She must have heard our conversation.

I didn't care what Martha thought. In my opinion the Holy Rule of the Sisters of St. Joseph was more humane than our Rule. They were allowed vacation, visited their families, conversed with each other during the day. Their convents were happy with laughter, and I saw smiling faces there. In contrast, our convents crackled perversely with the tension of silence as Sisters strained against the constrictions of human detachment.

Sister Joel's thin arms lovingly fastened around me, hugging me as if I were a long-lost and recovered friend. I easily forgot Martha's smothering paranoia. Joel and Daniel laughed like schoolgirls.

"Oh, there's much to tell you, Roseann." Their voices rose and fell. "We're just home from a workshop at the Motherhouse," Daniel said. "He was so exciting, Roseann, you couldn't believe it."

"Someone special?"

They both giggled. "Father Edward Barrett, the Titan, the one we all love now. Do you know him?" Joel asked.

"Barrett? Yes, yes," I said, feeling my breath stop for a moment. "He led us in a retreat in '56." Shamefully, I felt a sudden coldness toward them for having had what I had longed for. When I realized that I was punishing them for feeling the same things I felt for him, I placed my hand on Daniel's shoulders and drew Joel close to me.

"You should consider yourselves blessed." Their eyes sparkled. I wondered if he had kissed their hands as he had mine. But I couldn't hide my disappointment. Father Barrett had been so near, yet it might as well have been a thousand miles. I had feared to write him. The thought of having my letter to him and his reply read by my Superiors was a gift I would not allow them to steal.

"Take my notes," Daniel said softly. "He seems to mean a great deal to you."

Perhaps it was the will of God that Father Barrett only be allowed to visit me through his notes, his thoughts, and through the beauty of these young novices. While we talked, I watched them, realizing sadly that I had lost something very special—a freshness, or was it innocence?

I copied Father Barrett's notes slowly and secretly, savoring each thought and running my fingers over the words he had spoken. I carried his notes into chapel, reflecting on them: "Everything in the monk's life has meaning," he had said. "Especially the ancient woolen cowl. The *cuccula*, with its generous sleeves. Regard the hood," he said. "See how it protects, how it heals, how it offers the monk a haven from the tribulations of life. It provides a warm tent in the frigid desert of daily life where one may ponder, where one may meditate on the quirks, the fears which the world fires up so quickly and just as quickly squelches."

I could hear Father Barrett's voice as powerfully in that moment as I had years before. The urgent need to be healed within the folds of this holy cowl were soon followed by a deep sense of comfort and consolation as if he *had* wrapped me in the heavy brown woolen garb of the monk. It was almost as if I could feel the rough fabric of the hood touching my cheek; I felt warm, protected, and loved.

I had recruited Doreen Duffy, a young senior from Cathedral High School, a pixielike girl glowing with vital energy, to help me with my volunteer program. She had just turned eighteen, two years older than I had been when I entered the convent. One Saturday morning we sorted clothing together, stacking it in huge piles for distribution to the poor, disturbing hidden cockroaches, bringing back chilly memories of Harlem.

"I hate this," I said. "People suppose the poor have no dignity, that they'll take *anything*. They're treated as less than animals."

Doreen kept running to the bathroom to wash her hands. "Next time I'll wear gloves," she said.

I began looking forward to working with Doreen. When we met in the church basement, rather than the convent, we laughed and talked a lot. She shared the wonders of growing into womanhood, something I began to realize I had never experienced.

"You know, Sister Roseann, my mother thinks I'm unhinged hanging around here all the time," she said. "But I don't to be a nun. I just like being with you."

I teased her and rumpled her hair, feeling oddly thrilled at the physical contact. She looked at me with such openness I was taken offguard. For a moment we stood, the two of us, looking at each other. The one person I had really loved to be with before Doreen was Sister Judith.

For a moment I wanted to hug Doreen for just being herself. Instead, I held myself back, detached as I had been trained to be.

Doreen pratted on about her aunt; how she had dinner every Monday with her. "She is also my godmother," she bragged, and the warmth of her love touched me. I was reminded that my twin, Eileen, had just had her second baby daughter. Would I ever be able to give anything of myself to my nieces or would I be only a faraway, paperdoll-nun in their eyes?

"Sister Roseann, where do we put all this underwear?" Doreen called out.

"Let's start a new pile," I said.

"Sister, where were you just then?"

I laughed self-consciously. "Into dreams, impossible dreams, somehow."

She smiled and tilted her head at an odd angle that I found so endearing, then, mocking me warmly, she burst out, "To dream . . . the impossible dream."

Doreen and I continued working together in the parish each Saturday morning. Sadly, I admitted to myself that she brought more joy to my heart than my detached relationships with the Sisters, in which we were united in prayer and sacrifice but not in feelings.

One of those Saturday mornings when we had finished, Doreen dropped me off at the Department of Motor Vehicles, where lines of pushing people had gathered, snaking in and out. I thanked God this was only a yearly ordeal. I felt a tap on my shoulder.

"Roseann?" I turned. Jonathan was standing there beside me. I could feel his warmth radiating outward toward me. "You're always welcome in my home. You know that." I moved deeper into the milling crowd, trying to put some space between us. He followed closely behind, reaching me.

It had taken me months to control my emotions, to restrain my mind, my unholy self, from focusing on sexual pleasures, on the very act of making love. Yet I was learning to be stronger, perhaps a bit wiser and less judgmental about men's passions and about the feelings that drained my spirit and damaged my dreams of Sainthood.

I wanted to tell him, "I've visited your home a thousand times. I have been in your arms, held and let you hold me, kissed you and let you kiss me." But instead I said, "Please understand. I can't speak with you. I can hardly look into your eyes. I know you understand what I can't allow myself to say."

He bent closer to me. "More than you allow yourself to understand, Roseann. Don't punish yourself because I desired you. Don't crucify yourself because you're beautiful and have passion." He straightened up. "I wish you well, Roseann, and for what it's worth, I care for you. I won't leave your heart." Before I could move, he squeezed my hand and left.

I wanted to cry out, "Don't leave." But I didn't. The wound I thought had healed was torn open again. All that I feared was coming back. The desire of my flesh staggered me. Confession? Yes. It was not the answer, but it would be some release.

Father Ostoff listened patiently.

"Why did Jonathan have to come back? It wasn't my fault. If I made love just once, it would be over with," I said, shocked at myself for thinking it out loud.

"It is not the answer, believe me. It would make matters worse," he offered kindly.

"Father, if only I knew how to release the desire I feel. If there was something physical I could do."

When I left the confessional, I was as frustrated as when I had entered it. I began the Stations of the Cross angrily, pausing longer at the station where Simon of Cyrene helped Jesus carry His cross. It left a tight numbness in my heart. "You must let me go, Jonathan," I cried out in my darkness. "You must leave my thoughts."

Still, through this last meeting with Jonathan, I knew that something had been set right. Jonathan had heard my pain and guilt; he had said that he cared for me, said it with gentleness, not tauntingly, as he had before. He had acknowledged a bond between us that went beyond the sexual desire we were feeling for each other. I knew somehow that I should not need the consolation of human touching, human caring, but I did. Would I feel this terrible hunger for all the days of my life?

❦ 12 ❦

I felt that I had abandoned Jerome with my transfer from Ronston to Albany, and my constant prayers for his recovery did little to ease the emptiness I felt when I thought of him. Now I had a letter from Jean: "If you can manage it," she asked, "please visit Jerome. He still doesn't acknowledge me, but Dr. Ortiz has encouraged me to visit him often. Ortiz seems to be a marvelous doctor. He thinks that Jerome might perhaps recognize you and that could give Ortiz a way to reach Jerome. I haven't given up hope, Roseann, but it's been so difficult. Please, please, come."

I wondered how to approach Sister Martha to obtain her permission to visit Jerome. I was sure that she was aware of the events at Ronston, and of course she had read Jean's letter, but she never spoke of it.

Some nights when I did not sleep, I'd wander through the corridors inspecting my house work or looking out the attic storage room window at the stars. Early one morning, as the other Sisters still slept, I found myself on my knees in the hallway rubbing a spot I had missed in waxing the worn oak parquet floor. Something stirred on the edge of my vision, causing me to turn my head. I couldn't see clearly, but something seemed to be gathering itself, wisping near the door of my dormitory room. Before me, I saw a shadowy form. It seemed to be a garment of sorts, like a monk's habit. It was the dark brown woolen robe of a Franciscan priest, the cowl pulled up and forward, hiding a face—that wasn't there—in its shadows. I remembered the cowl that Father Barrett had described, remembered the feeling of the material against my own cheek, the feeling of being warm and protected under its covering. I was not afraid. This was an apparition of love. It seemed physically there as it took on increasingly clear physical form, and for an instant I knew that Father Barrett's spirit was with me.

I pulled myself up, smiling at this trick of vision. My back cracked as I rose; that was real enough. I blinked once, twice, but there was no film on my eyes. I was truly awake. I had been rubbing the floor. It was not real, but yet it was there.

I stared hard at it, expecting that it would disappear, but it didn't. Then I reached for the door, passing my arm through it, and even as I did, it faded like the heat that shimmers on highway asphalt only to dissolve. But I had felt something.

When I entered the dorm, Mariann was sitting on the edge of her bed, putting on her glasses, staring at me. "Roseann, is that you?"

"Yes."

She turned on the bedside lamp.

"What's wrong, Mariann?" I asked, trying to sound calm. "Is it too stuffy in here?"

"Something moved in the room," she whispered. "I felt something. It woke me. Was it you?"

"Did you see something at the door?"

"Yes, I thought . . . no . . . just felt something. Oh, I don't know." She got out of bed, looked around sleepily and started toward the bathroom.

I pulled the drapes tightly around my bed. I began to shake, and I wasn't able to calm myself. I tried to sleep, but my mind kept going back to whatever the apparition was. I had distinctly seen a monk's cowl. As I lay there in the dark,

I seemed to see Jerome's face emerge from the shadows cast by the cowl. I felt a secure, comforting presence. Could the monk's habit become a haven for Jerome? Was my vision a sign that the cowl was sanctuary for Jerome? I brushed the thought aside and finally drifted off to sleep.

When I awakened, the other Sisters were already in chapel. The vision of the night returned, stronger. It was not trickery or hysteria. It was real. It was no crazier an idea than Dr. Ortiz's painted altar, which had quieted Jerome's raving for absolution. Jerome had dreamed and had lived for the moment he would wear this habit to bless and heal his parishioners. It had now been denied him. The mere idea that I could help him made the presence of Christ rise in my heart. During Holy Mass I begged Jesus for answers, for assurance that this was indeed a mandate from Him.

When I spoke with Sister Martha, she seemed almost somber as she listened to everything I dared recount. "You seem to have a very vivid recollection of all these little incidents, but I find them hard to believe and there is no basis for accepting them."

"I don't mean disrespect when I say this, Martha, but I feel in my heart the idea is larger than me and even than your authority. I have prayed over this; it has taken me all morning to prepare myself for what I knew would be an unhappy encounter with you." The fact that this might not be the will of God was something I had rejected. For once, I had to go with what I felt to be true.

"Were you St. Joan of Arc herself, I would not give you permission to see Jerome. It's base presumption, a bloated ego, and your arrogance rather than your alleged love for Christ or for this unfortunate young man. How smugly you forget that God's will is made clear through *my authority*, not in your neurotic dreams. I cannot stop you physically from seeing him, but I warn you, Roseann, you have taken too much authority on yourself these days. It has not gone unnoticed. You are dismissed!" Her naturally ruddy face became even more flushed, and she pulled her sweater close around her like a suit of armor.

Madison State Hospital seemed almost cheerful in the summer sun, with trees in full foliage lessening the harshness of the institution's tan brick walls and barred windows. I walked slowly through the corridor of the ground floor, following the directions to Dr. Ortiz's office.

"I'm glad you've come, Sister Roseann," Dr. Ortiz said as he opened the door to admit me. I heard his soft Spanish accent, different from the familiar Mexican accents I had heard so often in my childhood in Los Angeles. I was surprised. Jean had not described him, and I had somehow assumed that he would be a tall, craggy, white-haired, venerable, old doctor. Here he was, just the opposite in every way. He was hardly an inch taller than I and we looked at each other at eye level. His straight, coarse hair was thick and black and as neatly trimmed as his thin black moustache. Smooth bronze skin seemed to fit tightly over the bones of his regular features, but his smile was warm and relaxed and was reflected in his eyes, which were truly startling. I would have expected them to be dark, but they weren't; they were light, an amber brown, even more startlingly framed in long black lashes. I did not think about whether he was handsome; it did not seem important.

"Does Jerome know I am coming?"

He motioned me to a chair. "Does Jerome know? Interesting question, Sister. He doesn't seem to know anyone. That's why I spoke to Jean. He may be closer to awareness of everyone and everything around him than we've been giving him credit for."

"I thank God for that, Doctor. I have so little to offer."

"You may have more to offer than you think." He glanced at my hands as they moved nervously over the brown paper-wrapped package I carried.

"Would you like a cup of coffee?" he asked as he moved toward a stained espresso pot that emitted a strong aroma.

"No, I don't drink coffee."

"Well," he said, "I believe it helps keep the brain cooking. Caffeine and humanity, my two addictions."

"Not such a medical approach, Doctor."

"No. Like most of my ideas, they aren't exactly acceptable around here." His face had darkened. "But in spite of what my colleagues claim, I believe Jerome has it in him to work through his psychotic episode. What I feel goes beyond the realms of psychiatric training. I don't have a so-called reality basis for believing that anything can work with him, Sister, but . . ."

"But you do have faith, don't you, Doctor?" He looked at me strangely, his lips parting. His expression was noncommittal, and I wished that I could read his mind.

Dr. Ortiz sighed deeply. "Faith is one of those words like *know*. We can spend the next ten thousand years discussing it. I hope, Sister, you believe me when I say my faith touches a greater understanding of how the whole ball of wax works, how we all fit into it." I nodded, not knowing what to say.

"I'm afraid it goes well beyond my Western conditioning or yours." He studied me intently and then walked to the window, looking up at the four towers that housed a thousand mental patients. He nodded his head pensively in their direction. "Most of these patients at Madison don't really belong here." He pushed past his wastebasket, nudging it with his foot. "It's a disgrace."

As he continued to talk, I hated my ignorance. I couldn't understand much of what he said, and I really couldn't begin to comprehend the strange and fearful world that Jerome inhabited. I could only listen.

"I envy you for one thing," he said sadly. "You can visit families in their homes, see exactly what's happening with them, what their emotional needs are, the root cause of their illness. At least you'd be able to offer a cure of sorts. This system," he almost shouted, "breeds diseased minds. Hospitals aren't the answer. They are, unfortunately, the easy solution. Lock them up and forget them." He dropped heavily into his chair, looking past me. For a moment his young, smooth face looked old.

"Are you a Catholic, Doctor?"

"I come from a long line of witch doctors." He laughed lightly for the first time since I'd entered his office. My feelings of insecurity, of inferiority, were disappearing. Slowly, I pulled my gift, a brown monk's habit with its large spacious cowl, from the paper wrapping. Dr. Ortiz threw his head back, his youthful look returning. "Is it your mission to turn me into a monk?" he chided easily, "or do you have some miracle in mind, young Sister, requiring a magic curtain?" It felt good to laugh.

I had conspired to borrow a habit from my young friend at St. Joseph's novitiate, Sister Joel, whose brother was a Franciscan priest. I didn't know how she explained to him why she wanted it.

"If you think my suggestion outrageous, I won't be upset. This habit, this cowl, may become a holy place, a safe place for Jerome."

"To hide in?" Dr. Ortiz asked simply.

"It is the habit he had longed to wear before he broke with our reality," I answered. I was afraid to mention my vision of the floating monk's cowl. "I find it hard to explain."

"Go on, Sister."

"It is quite possible that this cowl can heal his pain—pain in that place where Jerome is unable to free himself."

Carefully, the doctor lifted the brown woolen fabric, feeling its texture, putting it on, and lifting the large hood over his head, looking like a dark Latin monk except for his moustache. "I wonder . . . I wonder . . ." he mumbled as he took it off. "My great-great-grandfather grew old on the eastern flank of the Peruvian Andes. They called him Abendanengarl, witch doctor. Their secrets were never written, but handed from mouth to ear. As a child, I listened to their stories, these magic priests whose only church was the living rock. I studied their charms. Their success was mystical; it *was* magic." Now that he was not talking about Jerome, I noticed his body for the first time. He had the firm, hard muscles of an athlete with that strange quality of appearing relaxed and at the same time poised to spring into action. As he continued to talk, a warm glow radiated from his face. I couldn't take my eyes off him.

"When I was still an intern, I witnessed cures in the Central Quentana Roo Territory, south of Yucatan. I saw the natural mold composition we call penicillin. I saw herbal potions injected into the vagina that rendered young women sterile for two years without harm. I saw the mixture of herbs that the Gruyos said 'would cure cancer.' This was like a flick of my finger compared to the cures for the mind." Dr. Ortiz rubbed his eyes and sighed deeply. "Western medicine is not primitive enough in many respects . . . too slow to admit its rigidity. I won't give up my heritage, my tradition. You are right, Sister Roseann. This cowl, did you say St. Benedict's cowl?"

"No, I didn't."

"Oh, I thought you had. Never mind."

I had not said St. Benedict, even though it was strongly in my mind. How odd.

"The instrument, the magic, miracle, call it what you want, *is in the belief*. That is the key." He stood up again. "Sister, come with me."

We left his office and proceeded down a long hallway. Some of the padding in Jerome's cell was new, the old ruined by his mad clawing. The painted altar was as I had first seen it. Jerome sat crouched in a corner. Instinctively, I moved behind Dr. Ortiz, almost touching the back of his white smock. Jerome's eyes rolled back and forth as his head moved from side to side, keeping us both in view. When the cell door opened, I moved in behind Dr. Ortiz uneasily, clutching the cowl close to my own habit. Jerome had turned his back to us and I unraveled the habit, holding it suspended before him as solemnly as if it were a Bishop's cape.

"Jerome," I called quietly, "this holy habit will help you, will quiet the voices and heal your spirit. This holy habit, Jerome, through Christ, will bring peace and health to you."

He barely moved as he peered over his elbow. He had seen me, heard me. I lowered the habit onto the floor in front of him. Then Dr. Ortiz and I left his cell quickly and watched through the grated door. Jerome sniffed at the robe, rolled over into it, sucked at its sleeves. He repeated the ritual over and over until Dr. Ortiz reentered the cell and gently took the habit from him, saying softly, "I will bring this back tomorrow, Brother Jerome. Tomorrow."

Jerome whimpered as if something terribly precious had been torn from him.

Dr. Ortiz brought me a welcome glass of water. I found it hard to hold the glass, my hands were shaking so.

"Step one for your miracle, Sister." I wasn't sure how he meant it, then, as if reading my mind, he laughed. "I mean that as a joke. We've been through a rather dramatic set of circumstances. I'm sure that you're not used to being in the company of madness?"

"Am I not, Dr. Ortiz?" I found myself saying. "Nuns are not necessarily exempt . . ."

"The 'incipient madness factor,' my colleagues would call it," Dr. Ortiz said gently. "Yes, there is an element of madness that surrounds any area of repression, Sister, but . . ." and then, as if thinking better of it, he stopped.

"And faith, Doctor. Is there room for faith for one who's lost contact with it?"

"Faith is the key. Leading Jerome back to it will be my business here."

For the briefest moment I wanted to unload my battle-scarred emotions about Jonathan and the thorns tearing at my vow of chastity. Dr. Ortiz could show me how to release my emotions, where Father Ostoff turned me to the Stations of the Cross. I found myself biting my lip, a habit I had recently adopted. I said nothing, but walked with him down the long white-walled corridor to the car waiting outside.

When I returned to the convent from Madison State Hospital, Martha glared angrily at me as I opened the front door. "I won't waste my time telling you what I think of your disobedience or of your pride, Roseann. I promise you one thing. Mother Edmond will know, and I will take pleasure in what I plan to report to her." She stomped upstairs and banged her office door shut.

Disheartened, I stepped into the chapel and knelt in the back pew. Is it I who has gone mad, I asked Jesus behind the gold-veiled tabernacle? Is it worth this conflict, the doubt that God's will could be manifested through me in spite of my Superior?

The Sisters filed slowly into chapel for Rosary, and I watched each one genuflect, their eyes lowered through habit. To whom could I open my heart as I would to Judith? Perhaps Janice, I thought. At least I could trust her to keep her mouth shut. Mariann was too young, out of the novitiate only one year. The other Sisters were too paranoid of Sister Martha's surveillance. I ached for someone to confide in, Rule of Silence or no Rule of Silence. I had to. Father Ostoff had given his best in the confessional; sadly, his best was not good enough.

Just before night prayers, Sister Martha read the retreat list in a husky tone. I would be making the second retreat in August and Judith the first. Another year would pass without our being together to hide away in the garden and share and laugh, as I had dreamed of doing. Janice was being transferred, effective the following morning. Any chance of confiding in her was snatched from me. A sign from God? She looked elated; I wondered if they'd make her a Superior despite Martha's hatred and community politics.

As I looked about the community room at the Sisters' expressionless faces, I wondered if they really accepted the consequences of their vowed life without question. Although I could at times feel their struggle, how could I know what their real struggles were? We didn't know each other; we lived as strangers. Had any of them been sorely tempted against their vow of chastity as I had? Had they ever been kissed with passion or lost their virginity? No, they were all virgins, without a doubt. If we didn't have a Rule of Silence, a rule forbidding particular friendships, would we be friends, all of us? Could we know each other's secrets without making judgments? Would this take away from our devotion to Jesus? But this was not the Way of the Cross or the narrow road of our religious vowed lives.

Sister Martha announced that Sister Mariann would be taking courses at Catholic University, the same courses Ruth had taken. I bowed my head quickly so no one would catch my disappointment. Poor slow Mariann. Why had I been passed over? I had more seniority and greater needs. Sister Ruth had told me to have trust; the opportunity would come. At that moment her words sounded dull and empty.

Two weeks later I received a note from Dr. Ortiz: "Jerome wears his monk's habit twenty minutes each day. He treats his cowl as a dear old friend. Even addressed me as Dr. Ortiz for the first time in two years. It's my opinion that it's only a matter of time before his psychosis will be breached. Miracles do happen. I cannot thank you enough . . ."

Tears began to well up. I thought about some of the Sisters at the Motherhouse, nuns with vacant faces who came and went mysteriously. Janice told me they were sent out to heal in state mental institutions, then returned under the veil of secrecy, though priests went to the best private sanatoriums. There was something so uncontrollable, so horrifying about losing one's mind. In God's mercy I prayed I'd be spared such suffering.

When a refreshed Sister Martha returned from her retreat, she announced in a softer tone that Sister Janice had been appointed Superior of the Ronston convent. "Wonderful!" I said aloud. The Sisters laughed, though Sister Martha ignored the outburst. In the changes she reassigned me to

Holy Cross parish, a parish with too many illiterates and too many poor on welfare. The new assignment was cause to rejoice; for months I had longed to be needed in a parish. Also, it was a blessing to take me from St. George's, where the urge to see Jonathan sometimes became a maddening force that I feared I would never conquer.

Sister Martha was in rare form as she returned from retreat, even to the point of ignoring our house work. I was oddly aware of how loud her laughter had become when, on that quiet morning, she gathered the Sisters together in the community room. "I have a letter from Mother Edmond," she announced, and proceeded to read aloud: "'In accordance with the spirit of Our Holy Father, Pope John XXIII, the Vatican Councils, and modernization of Church rule, we will open a new Juniorate program this summer. Instead of the novices going directly to the missions as soon as they take their holy vows, they will spend four years longer at the Motherhouse and in college. I have appointed Sister Martha as Juniorate Mistress. She'll be responsible for the college and spiritual education of our newly professed Sisters.'"

This was truly happy news. I rejoiced for the young nuns coming up, but there was no word for the rest of us, who had been sent to the missions without a college education. Now, with Sister Martha directing the program, my chances of being included looked increasingly slim. Still, I had good reason to be happy this day. Along with the other Sisters, I congratulated Sister Martha with hearty and embarrassing jubilation. She was leaving our convent, great enough cause to kick up our heels and raise our voices in thanksgiving for God's infinite mercy. Indeed, Sister Martha had played her cards well with Mother Edmond and Mother had rewarded her with recognition. Martha's face glowed with the satisfaction of it.

After the milling about which followed, I found at my customary seat in the community room a small letter with Dr. Ortiz's now familiar script. I opened it carefully, as if something precious might spill and be lost among those who would not understand.

> Dearest Sister Roseann,
> Jerome speaks to me often these days. What he says could not be put in this letter. I feel it would be in his best interest if you could visit him again. I've enjoyed our exchanges and I miss your nourishing presence. The madness here gets no better. Phone me when you can set some time aside.
> > Ignacio Ortiz, M.D.

Perhaps my new Superior would allow it.

❦13❦

Our periodical and planned rotation of power was in process. Mother Cora, the Congregation's treasurer for the past twenty-five years, accepting humbly the will of God, was consecrated as the new Mother General. Mother Edmond's twelve-year reign ended, but not her influence. She now became Assistant Mother General. Her power would still be felt, though in subtler ways. Our new governing body was divided between conservative and liberal factions. By now the entire Order was aware of the Vatican's push for change, change that was penetrating the very walls of our cloister. The conservative Sisters, who were often but not always the older nuns, were strongly opposed to this movement toward modernization. The liberal and usually younger nuns, of whom I was an enthusiastic if somewhat fearful member, welcomed the changes and would have seen them implemented as speedily as possible.

Suspect philosopher, scientist-priest Teilhard De Chardin, so admired by my mother, became a recognized hero seemingly overnight. John Kennedy had caught the imagination of the world, and volcanic social change seemed everywhere. In this climate of uncertainty, Sister Ruth from Chicago, who months previously had introduced us to a course in theology, became our new Superior. No one was surprised.

Groomed in liberal thought, she swept in an attitude of love that she said "must be practiced in spirit and truth." We welcomed the change but not the confusion. Two ex-Superiors from our New York City convents arrived at the same time, Sisters Katherine and Rachel. The two Sisters had known each other for years and were possibly a cause of trouble because they had long been accustomed to the status of authority.

Sister Angelus came fresh from the novitiate, still wearing the constrictions of Coline's indoctrination. I remained Assistant Superior, understanding my "position" to be a passing status symbol, dampening my ambitious expectations of someday becoming a Superior.

Sister Ruth began classes in theology and the religious life as soon as she arrived. She never referred to notes and she always spoke with a quiet conviction that no one questioned. That she had come to us as Superior was more than I had hoped for. It was the answer to prayers I had feared to utter then. But now I thanked God for His kindness, for the grace-filled break that gave me hope that sainthood was not some dreamy illusion, that a sinner such as I could achieve holiness through the discipline of my vowed life.

After one of her classes, Ruth handed me a textbook, *Understanding the Five Senses.* "Study this book so you may teach it to the Sisters." She smiled kindly, and I felt embarrassed.

"Me? . . . teach? . . . these Sisters?"

She nodded her head, pushing the book into my tightly clasped hands.

"But, Sister, I'm not in touch with my own feelings. It's a joke. They will laugh at me. Ask one of the senior nuns. Please!"

"There was a time when I felt the same way, Roseann. Seniors can learn from the young; we all have grace and insight to share, regardless of age. It doesn't matter in the eyes of God. The process of teaching will aid you in understanding yourself. It will stretch you, because you need to be stretched. You have wonderful ability, Roseann. I'm not telling you to give the course, merely asking you. You are free to refuse." Her pleasant face widened in a patient smile as she waited confidently for my answer.

I flipped through the pages of the thin book and laughed. "I'll do it. It won't be the first time I've made a fool of myself."

"You have nothing to fear, Roseann."

Sister Ruth wisely scheduled my first class for the following afternoon.

"Sisters, our senses, our emotions, are friends we can embrace if we allow ourselves to understand them." The words flowed as if from an alien force, and I struggled to repress my feelings of hypocrisy. I had no right to be preaching a doctrine. After class I hurried out of the community room.

Before I turned the corner, I felt a warm hand on my elbow. "You are a natural teacher." Ruth beamed at me. "The challenge lies in your personal conviction, that your whole self, your senses, are your dearest friends." She spoke earnestly.

"But for twelve years I've been told they are my enemies, by holy women . . . by Mother General, by everyone except Father Barrett."

Ruth arranged her shoulder cape pushed out to parting around her well-rounded breasts, seemingly self-conscious of the full figure that even a nun's habit could not hide. She nodded. "He warned us about enforced ignorance, remember, Roseann?"

"I've tried to forget, I'm afraid."

"Don't forget. He was the unwanted prophet," she said.

"You're right, Ruth. If we had listened, change would come more easily for all of us."

"Easy? Hardly. Change is never easy. It means risks, touching the gray matter of the unknown. But I've gone through the same indoctrination you have, Roseann. Trust me. Trust in the changing Church."

"I didn't think the Church was supposed to change."

Ruth laughed lightly. "That's old-time ignorance. Only the dead don't change. You've been wearing blinders too long. Tear them off! Security founded on sameness is built on sand. We have covered our bodies, our minds, like the tunic that covered Lazarus. I tell you, rip the binding from yourself and for the first time you'll begin to taste true spiritual freedom, which is the joy of the Holy Spirit." Ruth's voice was strong and clear. None of the Sisters had moved from the community room. She had made her point for all of us.

For the rest of the afternoon Ruth's words repeated inside my head. What would happen if I allowed myself to be completely open, to experience my emotions to the limit? It terrified me. Could I handle the memory of Jonathan? Or the young Italian gardner who, in a fleeting moment, had dropped pansies in my lap?

Later that evening, when the third-floor bathroom was available, I decided to take a rare leisurely bath. It would be much longer than the prescribed ten minutes, I told myself. Slowly, I took off my veil and stood before the mirror. My hair resembled a half-grown-out crewcut. That's how Sister Maurice had cut it and forced me to keep it. I looked at my head closely. I thought I saw several silver hairs. I'm only twenty-eight! I almost spoke the words out loud. There were no lines in my face or neck. My skin was clear and fresh. I looked easily ten years younger than my age. I flexed an arm muscle. There appeared a soft swell. Once more I tried and stared, ashamed at its stringy weakness. My arms had been larger, tougher, in high school. I moved my fingers over my legs—still strong—as if they were foreign things, not living parts of me. How would I look in high heels, I wondered? I almost giggled. Funny, no doubt. In the moment I felt so alien to my physical self, the self I had once loved and trained for the Olympics. Why did I suddenly want to cry?

I dropped my long black robe, eyes closed tight. "Don't look at your private, sacred parts. Don't, lest your heart and mind be captured with impure desires," I taunted myself. I quickly reached to the wall for support. My eyes, distracted, shot to the mirror, to the forbidden vision of the naked body I had bathed thousands of times without ever really looking at myself.

I stared, breathing hard. I was a woman. Quickly, I jumped into the tub, sloshing water over the mat beyond the white tiles. Dare I be friends with this body of mine? The soap slipped unheeded through the bath water. No! I can't be too careful, I warned myself. Ruth was advanced in the spiritual life. I was not and that was a difference never to be underestimated.

Ruth had been Superior several months before she introduced us to the reading of secular magazines forbidden by Mother Edmond. She held a stack of them in her hands. "I'm keenly aware we have been saturated with our Mother Foundress's books and the many conferences of Mother Edmond, but we must keep up with the renewal thinking of the Church, with the events in our secular society, if we are to be shining lights." She placed them on the community room table, then added, "I am available for all of you. Please take advantage of the opportunity of confiding in me. I want to discuss anything that troubles you. Change will rattle the security we have become accustomed to. I understand the pain of change."

Several of the Sisters privately whispered about her disregard for tradition and the discipline of silence. We had become so ingrained to restraint, it was hard to believe this Superior wasn't another Sister Martha bent on burdening us with overbearing surveillance.

I spoke to Ruth after her conference in the small office opposite the community room. "In my heart I want to be part of the changing spirit in the Church," I said, "but it's more difficult because I don't see the administration supporting your ideas. You're too far ahead of them. I fear trouble. I fear, if these Sisters complain, you'll be transferred. We'll get a Superior worse than Martha, even a Maurice."

She touched my hands gently. "Perhaps you're right, but someone has to wear the shield of courage, take the risk, pay the price, as did our Mother Foundress in the days when she established our Congregation. She was terribly misunderstood then. But if she had not believed in what her mission was, this wonderful community of Social Work Sisters would not be here today. Understand?"

I nodded. In Ruth's presence I felt relaxed and delighted. She trusted me. I felt understood, though I failed to understand myself.

During the first six months of Ruth's administration, the most distrusting Sisters had begun to give her a graceful half chance. Former Superiors Katherine and Rachel took the attitude of "wait and see." I liked the change of being asked to do things and not told; of being encouraged to read without feeling guilty that I was being self-indulgent or wasting time.

It was winter. Ruth and I drove through a snowstorm to the Motherhouse to bring newly professed Sister Sheila to our convent. I was waiting in the Motherhouse's foyer when Sister Martha stopped me.

"How have you been, Roseann?" she asked.

"Things have been much better lately," I said. Then, ashamed of what I had intended to be a cutting reply, I asked, "How is the Juniorate program going?"

She lowered her voice. "If Edmond were still Mother General, we'd be making real progress. Mother Cora is weak and doesn't have the experience. She can't make simple decisions, and the novices coming out of the novitiate are not prepared. It's Coline's fault; she needs to be replaced as Novice Mistress."

I was shocked at her open criticism. Just that moment Coline passed through the foyer; both mistresses exchanged cold glances. It was rumored that Martha had turned liberal, an incredible turnabout. It must have been in reaction to

Coline, who, rockbound in conservative tradition, was not bending with the Church's renewal.

I was relieved when Ruth gestured for me to meet Sister Sheila. It was rumored that her first vows had been delayed because Coline wasn't convinced she had a "true religious calling." But I knew Sheila had entered the Order with a degree in education, which spared her four years longer at the Motherhouse in Martha's Juniorate program. As I shook her hand, I looked up at the serious countenance of a twenty-four-year-old, six-foot two-inch woman from France. She was impressive, very beautiful and strangely solemn.

Back at our convent, I noticed that Sheila's private conferences with Ruth, which had been once a week, increased to twice weekly. During meals, Ruth had become extraordinarily attentive to Sheila, who never left Ruth's side.

Although aware of Ruth's increasing preoccupation with Sheila, I dismissed it with the presumption that it was because Sheila was younger than the rest of us and so newly professed in her vows.

When I returned from the parish one evening, I went to my dormitory to change my clothing, drenched from the heat that seemed to cling to the black wool habits. I heard voices coming from the attic storage room above. I realized that Ruth and Sheila must have assumed that was a place they could talk without being overheard.

"But my Novice Mistress never accepted me, Ruth. She never did. She wouldn't even give me my mother's ring. She hates me; that's why she postponed my vows. It had nothing to do with the validity of my religious vocation. The administration is threatened by anyone who questions their authority. None of these Sisters like me. I feel it. Especially Roseann."

"Come now, Sheila," Ruth cut in. "Roseann gets along with everyone."

For an instant I felt a wave of kindness toward Ruth for

taking my part and distrust for Sheila, whom I thought I had always treated kindly.

In the weeks that followed, Ruth's office door was closed more often to all the Sisters except Sheila. I was thrown into a whirl of confusion, trying not to judge them, to practice patience, whatever it took. My parish work drew me out of my brooding until I returned to the convent, where every doubt I had been battling was perched at the convent gate.

One evening as I passed through the community room, Ruth waved me to come in. "Would you mind helping me move my desk?"

I grabbed the end of it and pushed it out of the room. "Getting a new one?"

"No, just putting it into Sheila's room."

We moved the small desk to the far corner, and I noticed that Ruth had also moved her bed into the room. Sheila, folding her laundry, avoided looking at me. It took enormous effort to control the anger I felt at this exclusive relationship. As Assistant Superior I was expected to give unquestioning loyalty, not merely to fill in for Ruth when she wasn't available, which had become quite often these past weeks.

When I went to the laundry room to gather my ironing, Rachel and Katherine were at my side, pressing me to the wall. "Something must be said to the administration about this situation with Ruth and Sheila," Rachel said, her steel-blue eyes holding mine, her anger close to the surface.

"What do you mean?" I asked, knowing exactly what she meant.

"Come on, Roseann," Katherine said. "You're not stupid. It's a scandal—Ruth and Sheila sharing a room. They miss prayer; they miss meals. You do all Ruth's work. It's a disgrace," she added.

"You'd better give Ruth a warning," Rachel broke in. "Tell her she'll be replaced as Superior. You'll report her to Mother Cora. Sheila will be thrown out of the community.

You're Assistant Superior. It's your responsibility. You owe it to the rest of the Sisters," Rachel said, twisting her rosary beads. As both Sisters spoke they kept moving closer to me until I felt I was being crushed.

"I need time to think before I take it upon myself to make any accusations to Ruth."

"No one accused them of anything, Roseann," Katherine said, almost too gently.

I looked away, hating them for putting me in this position. "I think both of you had better leave," I said. And they did. Who could I turn to? Judith? Phone her? My confessor? My God! Who was there to talk to?

It was with great reluctance that I confided in Father Ostoff, who hunched closer to the confessional curtain than I could ever remember. There was a long, painfully long, silence. "Sister, I do suggest you voice the Sisters' concerns; but as you're aware, no one has proof of what goes on behind their closed door," he added.

"That's right." I breathed easier. When I left Father Ostoff, I knew I had to speak to Ruth. I was run ragged doing her work, correcting the Sisters' parish work, filling in for her every day. It was wearing me down. Worse still, there wasn't a corner in the convent that someone wasn't using to gossip. I was sick of it.

When I returned to the convent, I picked up our mail. There was a letter from Dr. Ortiz. I opened it and read it there without taking it to Ruth first. He was again asking me to call, to visit Jerome. For the first time, I did not ask for a Superior's permission.

❦ 14 ❦

Dr. Ortiz stood by the sunlit window of his office observing me critically. "You look as if you haven't slept well lately. Sit down please."

I folded myself deeply into a leather chair that seemed to draw months of pressing tension from my body. "I am tired," I found myself admitting. "Tired of myself, I suppose."

He pulled a chair over close to mine and sat down. "Roseann, I wonder if your needs are any less serious than Jerome's. Relax. He will be cared for in due time." His smile warmed me and I wished that he could put his arms around me and hold me. The comfort and understanding promised by his attention was too much for me to resist. I was suddenly unloading my confusions and frustrations about knowing and accepting God's will, about Jonathan, about Ruth and Sheila, spilling it out in a maze of tangled words and tears. "I was afraid to come here until today. There is something so terrifying about Jerome's madness. I don't want to feel it. I confess, I'm afraid to be a part of it."

Dr. Ortiz leaned closer and I could feel his breath brush across my face as he massaged my hands lightly. "You know, you are not the little girl you cling to who once made you feel so safe and secure."

"Maybe you're right." I turned my face and wiped my eyes.

"You are a woman ripe with emotions, desires, budding life, something this Jonathan felt and, no doubt, wanted to share. I can hardly blame him. It's nothing you should fear or hate; it's part of your wholeness."

"But my vow of chastity?" I hung my head, afraid to look at him.

He lifted my chin lightly. "Look at me, please. Jerome is mad because he can't deal with repressed emotions demanded by his religious order. It has driven him into a world where he feels safer with 'monsters.' You see, he is suffering in his mind what I suspect you are suffering in your soul. There is really little difference. But you are correct in fearing the madness, for in it is buried truth."

I stared at him, astonished. He had drawn from me the hurt I couldn't bare to admit to myself and had explained it in terms I could appreciate and understand. "I'm afraid of this insanity, of losing my mind."

"Because you can't control what you feel?" he asked evenly.

"Yes, in my life as a nun."

"And?"

"What more is there?"

"Your religious life, your home, the place where you live, the family that supports you, the grounding that we humans in this vast chaotic world seek to give ourselves a sense of root," he said.

"I find myself uprooted, always uprooted. Everyone I love is taken from me. Then I am told that I am forbidden to love them, that they are forbidden to love me. But I do have Jesus," I added with pathetic courage. I stood up, hoping to find some strength in standing.

"Can you feel Him? Can you? You can't touch Him. You can't make love to Him, Roseann!"

My body convulsed in spasms of unrestrained sobbing. Now Dr. Ortiz gently took me into his arms as I had wished

Beverly Hills Public Library
Return Receipt

Title: Holy terror : Andy Warhol close up / Bob
Colacello
ID: 35048003813043

Title: These few precious days : the final year
of Jack with Jackie / Christopher Andersen
ID: 35048005561243

Title: Death and disaster : the rise of the
Warhol empire and the race for Andy's millions /
Paul Alexander
ID: 35048002859799

Total items: 3
12/3/2013 6:51 PM

Circulation Department
310-288-2222

he would do, running his hands over my shoulders until the sobbing passed.

"So it's not losing your mind that really troubles you, is it, Roseann? Your sanity is fine, I feel. You're a strong person. But I'll tell you now that if you don't find a proper release for your emotions, for your mental and spiritual life, your health will suffer."

"I'm stronger than that."

"And you can take anything?" he added sardonically.

"Yes, *anything!*"

"In the name of Christ? In the name of the Church? Have you thought, Roseann, that the life of a nun is a little too demanding? That maybe it's not the path for you if you keep tormenting yourself?" He turned his back then and I knew he was giving me time to collect myself.

"I have vowed my life to Christ, Dr. Ortiz, and to the service of His Church."

He turned quickly, his eyes narrowing. "Because you want to be a saint and martyr yourself for souls."

"It's not what you suppose. I'm not a quitter. My religious life is meant to be the Way of the Cross, not a bed of roses."

"Why not?" He fell silent.

I dried my face with the end of my sleeve, self-consciously. "We seek the road of sainthood," I added.

"And how do you release this sainthood?"

"By good works, by caring, loving."

"Aha! Release? Do you masturbate?" He grinned slightly. "It's a marvelous release. Beats running, you know, besides being tremendously pleasurable."

I found myself heading for the door. "It is a sin," I shouted.

"Now, now, Sister," he said, holding my shoulder gently. "I didn't intend to offend you."

"But you did mean to shock me."

"A minor shock. Don't you see how your Sisterhood demands you wear armor of steel and how it chafes one so sensitive? I'll tell you what sin is. It is guilty repression, the stick religion beats you with, controls you with. Witch doctors know about such things." His eyes had grown sad. I looked away, unwilling to continue the subject.

"Jerome. How is he?"

"Making progress, good progress. Listen to this tape. It will give you a feeling, an understanding about the nature of his illness."

I closed my eyes, trying to concentrate.

The tape clicked on. Suddenly loud riotous sounds, which I recognized as fists pounding on cell walls, exploded into the room. There was a moment of quiet and then Jerome's voice:

"I am the Lord God," he announced. "Oh yes I am. The Lord God speaks," he called out in a high, unnatural quivering voice. "And I have always been the Christ, as I am, as you see me, on my head, my elbows, beneath me, through my fingers, on my tongue. I am the infallible One, the All-powerful. Kneel! Aha . . . Ortiz . . . I can strike you down with my little finger. Twist . . . twist . . . and Henry's neck is off . . . ha . . . ha . . ." There was a garbled sound, then Jerome lapsed into rumbles of eerie laughter, as if it had been recorded in a tin shack.

"Shut it off, please. I don't want to hear any more."

Dr. Ortiz stopped the recorder calmly. "It gets better," he said. "He actually gets into transforming himself into different galaxies and glowing meteors. But he has changed."

"Can I see him?"

"Yes, but understand that while you think that Jerome's madness is blasphemy, I've listened to him many times. What he says isn't all that insane."

I looked at him, puzzled.

"Roseann, certainly you must understand what Jerome cries out for."

"No. I really don't understand what you mean."

Dr. Ortiz rocked his chair in a slow and easy motion, reminding me for an instant of Father Barrett who, in his own ponderings, had made the same physical motion.

"Jerome says he is God. Isn't that what your Church teaches? We are Gods, in the Mystical Body of Christ? What we do to each other affects the whole. Jerome has carried this notion to the extreme. We all want to acknowledge being a God, be it saint, nun, or doctor. We just don't shout it from the house tops." He grinned.

"I won't argue the point," I said.

"It's been some time since you've given him the cowl."

"And he has made steady progress, hasn't he?" I found myself saying.

Dr. Ortiz merely looked at me. "Come, please." We walked silently until we came to a small orchard behind the furthermost wall of the hospital grounds. The doctor moved off to the side, leaving me to stand and gaze at a slim young man dressed in brown pants and a yellow shirt, healthier looking than I had ever seen him.

Without a sound, Jerome turned and faced me and bowed ever so slightly from the waist. I moved closer to look into his clear eyes. Tears were beginning to form in my eyes.

"I'm not completely well yet," he said softly, "but if I could kiss the inside of your heart I would, and offer you thanks for your healing prayers." He took a step forward, lifted my hands, and kissed them tenderly. I couldn't speak.

He reached into a paper bag and pulled out the monk's habit. "I do remember the day you gave this to me." Jerome gazed at me earnestly. "I remember every word you spoke then. I felt your love, and my life will be too short to thank you for your caring."

I swallowed and looked toward Dr. Ortiz, who smiled shyly. I was too stunned to think clearly.

"I'll be leaving the hospital for my first home visit." Jerome beamed.

"I'm happy for you. I wish you every happiness and peace." Weak as it was, it was all, I was able to say. I found myself standing on my toes to kiss him lightly on his forehead and then watched as he walked off.

Dr. Ortiz moved to my side. "Why didn't you tell me?" I asked.

"Your reaction, in this way, was what Jerome needed for his healing. Don't you understand? He needed to see your tears, to feel your emotion, to have you forget yourself long enough to touch his face with a gentle kiss, from a woman, a woman of God." Now I wept openly.

He walked with me to the car. "My residency here will be over at the end of this month. I'll be returning to Lima." He paused. "Perhaps that's why I pushed you further today. I will miss you in ways I'm unable to tell you."

"You mean a man of your profession is unable to express feelings?" I asked lightly in spite of the deep sadness I felt at his leaving.

"May I write to you sometimes, and will you answer? I want to know how you are doing." As I nodded, he put his arm across my shoulders and pulled me briefly against him.

"Witch doctor," I whispered. "I won't say good-bye."

As I drove away, I thanked God for Dr. Ortiz. He had given me strength to face what awaited me back at the convent. From the convent garage as I parked the car, I could see Sister Katherine hurrying toward me.

"Have you spoken to our dear Superior?"

I shook my head. "I plan to. Tomorrow."

"It better be." She stormed off.

Gathering my courage, I stopped Ruth as she left the room she shared with Sheila.

"Sister?" I called to her.

She looked at me impatiently. "Important, Roseann?"

"Very." She studied my face as I tried to find words. "The Sisters have approached me with their concerns recently." I paused awkwardly. "I mean the fact you're not available to them." There was no stopping now.

Ruth stiffened her back as I went on. "That you're . . . involved with Sister Sheila." My stomach had begun to twist so tightly that I ached to sit down.

"Why haven't they complained to my face?" Ruth demanded.

"But, Sister, your door is never open. Sheila seems to need all of your attention. It gives scandal. No one understands." By now my own frustration was carrying the conversation. "Certainly you can understand how the Sisters feel, the way you used to be and now this." I tried to soften my voice. "What I mean is that you've changed, the convent isn't the same anymore. It's worse in some respects than Martha's Superiorship. At least we knew where we stood with her." I regretted speaking my mind so thoroughly.

"You have no right, no right to pass judgment on me or Sheila. I'll tell the Sisters what I think of their suspicions. Ring the bell! Now!"

My head was clearer than it had been for weeks. Confronting Ruth had been as much Katherine and Rachel's responsibility as mine, and after the fact, I painfully realized this. Now it would be me Ruth would distrust.

"What I plan to say, Sisters, will take precious little time. It is a sacred precept to mind one's own business." Ruth's voice was hard. "And it has been brought to my attention that a spirit of discontent has risen among the lot of you because you have judged what I do and how I do it. '*Thou shalt not judge and thou wilt not be judged,*'" she quoted, and with each precise word she spoke, she reestablished the power of her authority on the word of God. She stormed from the community room with Sheila close behind.

I felt a tap on my shoulder, and Katherine whispered, "You'll have to go to the Mother General. It's the only thing left to do."

I spun around. "That's what you think! Take your complaints to Mother Cora if you want your kind of action."

She backed off.

The following Monday after spiritual reading, Ruth took me aside. "Mother Cora is transferring Sheila to Milwaukee." Her face was ashen. Her grief was terrible to see.

"I'm sorry," I said simply, and walked away. I wished I had more to offer.

I remembered in pain when Ruth had given us her first theology class, when she had brought joy, freedom, and intellectual growth to this convent as our Superior. This was somehow the cruelest blow of all. Ruth would never again be a trusted teacher, admired leader. She would never hold a position of authority and respect. She had broken the Holy Rule against personal attachments between Sisters. Was the Holy Rule right? Did we really have to give up human attachments in order to serve God and His Divine Son, Jesus?

ST. ANTHONY'S CONVENT
New Haven, Connecticut

♥ 15 ♥

A few weeks later, Ruth was reassigned. Sister Arlene, a seasoned Superior, had been named to replace her. Arlene
moved quickly to heal the wounds in our convent. I sat with
her that first day, trying to be painfully discreet about Ruth
and Sheila. What Arlene knew, she never revealed. We
spoke in hushed tones as other Sisters anxiously waited in
the community room to speak with her. They thought they
needed to make favorable impressions to win her good
graces. It was a matter of survival for the months to come. I
had one consolation; new assignments had been made and I
was secure in Albany for another year.

I liked Sister Arlene. She seemed stable, her stability
earned, I thought, by her forty years—twenty spent as a
nun. I hadn't been reappointed Assistant Superior. I sus-
pected Mother Cora wanted Sister Arlene to work with
someone who hadn't been associated with Ruth. It seemed
that I was now tainted. Politics!

Sister Arlene had been Superior just five weeks when she
informed me I was being transferred to New Haven, Connecticut. She had no explanation, but tried to console me.
"You'll do fine at St. Anthony's Convent. It's the best catechetical mission we have."

"That's not the point," I said. "I'm doing fine here. All transfers were made weeks ago."

She shook her head sadly. "Go to the chapel. Ask the Sacred Heart for His help. I don't have any answers."

And she expected *me* to find some!

St. Anthony's Convent on Willow Street was large, with eleven private bedrooms, a large bathroom, and an office, all on the second floor. For the first time in fourteen years I had a double-spring mattress bed, not a wire cot. It felt new. Each room had a sink, dresser, mirror, and large closet. I sucked in the air deeply. How luxurious! On the bottom windowpane was a two-by-four-inch card: "Pull shade down." I looked outside. Lord! It was the rectory. It would be strange living in the same parish I worked in with the priests as neighbors.

Sister Lisa, the Superior, as Sister Martha's former assistant and protégée, had once been my unseen nemesis. Now she waved to me from her office. "I hope you'll like it here. If you need anything, let me know." She laughed lightly, standing as tall and as slender as I.

I guessed that she was about ten years older than I, although her rather too sharp and too thin features may have made her look older. Her attitude seemed relaxed enough, not the tense, rigid person I had expected. I was glad for my first feelings of comfort with her in spite of the misery Sister Martha had inflicted on me by repeated comparisons between Lisa's perfections and my imperfections.

Six Sisters worked in St. Anthony's catechetical parish and the other four Sisters, called the Toluca Team, worked exclusively for Father Galliano, the director of religious education for the archdiocese. The team traveled around the archdiocese giving workshops on how to teach catechism to public school children. They went every summer to Catholic University and were regarded by our community as the "Rolls-Royce Educators." Needless to say, I had already begun thinking about working with the Team.

However, in my first assignment I was expected to run the religious instruction program at John Adams School in the center of a tight-knit community of old-time Italian families. Sister Lisa observed my work initially and thereafter never directed or interfered with what I did. Soon I became complacent in my freedom, like a contented harbor seal, thinking this blissful state would last forever. It did last until one evening after spiritual reading Sister Lisa made the announcement that Sister Martha would be spending some time with us. "She'll work with our Toluca Team." Heads lifted; a few half smiles passed from Sister to Sister, an exchange of secret signals for which I had not yet learned the language.

Clara and I went down to the basement to whisper. It was easy to talk with her since we had been in the novitiate together. "Why do you think Martha's coming here? She's the Juniorate Mistress," I asked.

Clara had just returned from the Motherhouse and was privy to its gossip. "Oh come on, Roseann, you know as well as I do," she grinned. "I've heard she's close to a nervous breakdown, all that fighting with the Novice Mistress and her attitude toward Mother Cora. It probably got the best of her."

"I guess," I said. "But coming here! Sweet Jesus. I don't like the idea. I lived with her as my Superior. Lord!"

Clara raised her eyebrows. "What do you have to worry about? She'll be working with me."

"You have my sympathy," I added. "Who's going to run the Juniorate program in the meantime?"

"Sister Henry."

I remembered her as a proud and imperial-looking woman. She was editor of our Order's magazine and was seen frequently in the company of Mother Cora and Edmond. Yes, she was being groomed for bigger things. Clara and I heard footsteps on the basement stairs and moved away from each other.

While we recited the litany of the Blessed Virgin during

night prayers, I thought of Martha and Coline. How well I knew them both. The hot-tempered Italian Coline versus the tight, rigid German Martha—turned liberal. How ironic, I thought, that it was Martha who broke first.

A bundle of raw nerves, Sister Martha arrived at St. Anthony's Convent like a volcano. Behaving as if she were still Lisa's Superior, it took just three days for the anger to erupt. As I stretched, secretly flexing my arms, thighs, and buttocks while I dusted the hall baseboards, loud voices from the dining room broke the inner quiet I sought to master.

"You're back in the Dark Ages, Lisa," Martha shouted, "telling me how to run my schedule. The Toluca Team isn't your province. You remind me of the nerve of a conniving friar!"

Lisa's voice was strained. "I have studied the Vatican encyclicals and it's my understanding—"

Martha cut in, "*Understanding?* You don't even know how to shepherd a convent. The Sisters talk; they complain about your backward ways!"

"Martha, lower your voice, please!"

"Are you afraid of who will hear the truth, Lisa?" Both nuns edged out into the hall where I stood. Martha's face was scarlet; Lisa's was chalk white. She left Martha, talking to herself, and headed for the kitchen.

Lisa was alone in the kitchen, tears dripping on the potatoes she tried to scrub. My first instincts were to hug her, tell her to "forget the bully." Instead, I asked, "Do you need any help?"

She didn't look up. "Thank you. I can manage. I'm fine."

But she wasn't fine. Every day for twenty-eight days Martha battered Lisa with the whip of her ugly tongue. Our once peaceful convent turned into a vicious storm center, witnessed helplessly by the Sisters. Lisa tried to protect those of us who would have supported her by refusing to let us get involved.

In an early gray dawn, I watched from my bedroom window as Lisa, eyes red and swollen, put her small trunk in the car and drove off alone without a word.

I went about my work in the parish filled with hate for Martha. I couldn't get back to the convent fast enough. When I opened the convent door, the bell was ringing, Sisters moving quickly to the community room. We stood at our places, waiting. Then Sister Judith appeared from the office to take her place where Lisa had always sat. I blinked. Judith, my Judith, here! "Sisters, I have a letter to read from Mother Cora. Please be seated."

"'My dear Sisters in Christ,'" she read. "'I have appointed Sister Judith as Superior of St. Anthony's Convent, replacing Sister Lisa, who has been reassigned. I ask God's blessing on each Sister as she carries out her assignments responding generously to the will of God.'"

When Judith finally was free from all the Sisters hovering about her, I took her hands. "Thank God you've come. It's been a scandal," I added. "It makes me cold inside to see what can happen to women of God."

Judith studied me intently. "Religious life is by no means perfect. Human nature is fallible. But Sisters are striving to be perfect and that is the difference. You must not forget that, Roseann." She hugged me. "I am glad we are together. It's been a long time."

With Judith to talk to, my parish work and convent life were bathed in warmth. One day she brought good news. "I thought you would like to know that Lisa is going to Fordham University for her master's degree in religious education."

This served as a painful reminder of how much I also wanted an education and how many times I had been passed over in favor of both older and younger Sisters. I approached Judith with the problem. "I need to take courses, begin somewhere, achieve in a way that will give me fresh ideas, or my whole life will pass before I've had a chance," I said breathlessly.

Judith rubbed the edges of her fingers, knobbed by arthritis. "Sit down, Roseann. You make me nervous, quivering there like a hummingbird in flight." I laughed.

"And what kind of courses have you been contemplating these days, Roseann?"

I thought of Jerome, of Dr. Ortiz. "Psychology. That's what I want to major in. I have the need."

Judith beat a clicking tune with the end of her pencil on her desk. "I know a friend of Father Galliano, a Dr. Peters, professor at Yale. I'll give him a ring."

I waited in chapel, trying to calm my excitement by moving my fingers over my rosary beads—many turned brown with age. I smiled to myself. Brown beads were an obvious sign of seniority, separating us from the young Sisters with their shiny black beads.

Judith was able to arrange for me to enroll in a psychology course given by Dr. Finkelstein. I had missed the first two lectures. When I walked into his class, largely attended by adults, I felt awkward, a nun among so many men in this unfamiliar college classroom. Dr. Finkelstein lectured energetically on the workings of the brain, striding up and down, leaping into the air from time to time in grand theatrical style. He was the star. As he performed, I struggled to understand.

He passed out a twenty-question multiple-choice test and afterward called me to the front of the room. "Your test, please."

"But this is my first class."

"That isn't my problem, now is it?" Every item was wrong. "Take a seat please, Sister. Relax. This isn't Spain in the fifteenth century, after all. I'm not the Grand Inquisitor out to execute you!"

Red-faced, I returned to the rear of the room. The next class came too soon. At the end of class, Dr. Finkelstein gave me another F.

"Drop the course, Sister. It's nothing to be ashamed of, but you can't cut it."

My throat ached. "Give me one more chance, please, one more. You'll see a change, I promise."

Dr. Finkelstein adjusted his glasses. "Okay, just one more chance. Understand?"

"Judith, do you think I can do it?" I asked when I described it later.

"Certainly," she said. "You can do anything you set your mind to."

I tore into my study. Learning how to study was the real problem, I told myself before I attacked the textbook.

A week later Dr. Finkelstein poised his red marker, checking the first column of my test paper once, then twice. "Hummm . . . well I'll be damned." With a flurry of showmanship and three dance steps, he printed *B*, large and clear. The students broke out in wild crazy cheering and Dr. Finkelstein's face cracked slightly.

Judith beamed when I showed her the paper. "Well, I guess that will show them." I didn't know whether by them she was talking about the school or the Order. It really didn't matter which. I suddenly felt that I could show them all.

During this time I received my only letter from Sister Ruth:

Dear Roseann,
   I have been seeing a psychiatrist in New York City, but he doesn't seem to understand my needs. My Superior is against me. Sheila wants to visit me. She writes me every day. The Congregation made a terrible, serious mistake in rejecting her for final vows.

It was a sad letter and I couldn't bear to read it over. I tore it into small pieces, watching despondently as they fell into the wastebasket.

A week or two after I successfully finished my psychology course, just as I was almost out the door for John Adams School, Judith stopped me. "You're going to Catholic University in Washington, D.C., this summer with the Toluca Team to take the teacher training course," she blurted out.

"I can't believe it. I had given up hope. Mother Cora consented?"

Judith shifted her weight from side to side. "Just a matter of reminding Cora that it's about time our senior Sisters get a few breaks—simple justice when you think of the opportunities the junior Sisters get."

Days skipped and leaped as I prepared to leave for Washington.

There was a moment when Judith filled my trunk with reference books. "Just in case the library is limited."

"Limited? At Catholic University?" I asked.

"Perhaps not limited, but these are familiar. They will be your friends in a place where everything is strange. These books will comfort your spirit quicker than books that come to you cold from an alien shelf. Study hard," she added. "And in the name of God, enjoy yourself."

♥ 16 ♥

The Toluca Team, Sisters Clara, Norma, Margaret, and Adele, were well seasoned and regarded me as not tested enough for the "eagles' cliff." I felt keenly mixed sensations of fear and excitement when we arrived at Catholic University. I was anxious to learn, to be a shining witness of my Christian religious vocation. A sea of nuns, priests, and brothers fanned out neatly in registration lines for their graduate classes and special workshops. By the time I checked off three courses—theology, teaching methods, and leadership training—I was less insecure.

The "new nuns," Sisters of St. Joseph, Notre Dame, Religious of the Sacred Heart, and so many more, once garbed in long black habits, wore dresses or trim suits with skirts just below their knees. They were feminine, with veils pushed back, exposing their hair. They drew attention of those of us still garbed in traditional floor-length habits, but especially the attention of the male religious, their eyes drawn to uncovered legs and shapely breasts.

The five of us were scholastic orphans on our own. How we worked, prayed, and took our classes was our own responsibility. I had no Superior to answer to. I was in charge of myself. Even so, I envied the progress of the "new nuns," so far ahead of us in their modernization and the renewal of their Holy Rules.

On campus, priests said Mass in the classrooms on the grounds with nuns strumming guitars. We sang "Blowin' in the Wind" and "We Shall Overcome." Exhilarated with the new English Liturgy, we hugged and gave each other the "kiss of peace," and it felt good to touch and be touched in the love of Christ.

Catholic University's population encompassed the traditionals, the moderates, and the liberals alike. It pulsated with life. Traditional doctrines were being challenged in my theology class, taught for the first time by a nun theologian, Sister Juliette.

I wanted to be a twentieth-century modern Christian witness, particularly when I noticed the new nuns and priests huddle together conversing in soft, intimate tones. Nuns had always been invisible in comparison with the revered position of priests in the Church. Now, with their renewal and updated Holy Rules and their championing of social causes, the old caste system was changing.

Beliefs I had held sacred all my life were being challenged. The ban on eating meat on Fridays had been abolished and, with it, many items from the list of mortal sins. Fish was suddenly tastier. The spirituality of the laity was becoming as precious as our own religious callings. We were no longer holier by nature of our vocation as nuns, because each vocation was the living expression of love in the Church.

We had been taught since childhood that nuns and priests were special, holier, set apart; heaven was ours, without a doubt, because we had given up everything to follow Christ. This change troubled me gravely, because I didn't understand how something as serious as this could possibly change. Without it, what was the point to our life of sacrifice?

The critical mind I had repressed at age fifteen was returning quickly. I pushed back my veil a full inch, showing my hair, a simple way of proclaiming that I wanted to show I was visibly a part of the changing Church.

Sister Adele, my Tuluca Team roommate, cautioned me, "Better pull your veil forward, Sister. Our Holy Rule hasn't been abrogated yet!"

I laughed. "Who will I hurt here?"

"Yourself," Adele replied. "And in ways you won't understand until it's past the time of redemption." She walked away stony-faced. I didn't push it forward.

Priests, nuns, and laity were crowding through the rough-hewn stone doors in the field house building for Sister Juliette's lecture on "Changing Theology." It was both the topic and the professor that drew the crowds, many carrying briefcases, notepads, and tape recorders, something conspicuously missing in the other classes.

Sister Juliette displayed her hard-earned authority and expertise with razor-keen sharpness and she did it proudly. Nearly six feet tall, she wore full lay dress, offset by a delicate silver cross hung loosely around her long, graceful neck. The way she moved made me wonder if she had once been a dancer. Her long wavy black hair was unlike the short nun styles common on campus. Her luminous dark brown eyes, once seen, were not easily forgotten. But more than this, she accurately aimed an intellectual whip at her target, be it ignorance or complacency.

After one class, she grabbed two overflowing briefcases and headed down the long corridor.

"Wait," I called. She slowed a little and turned, smiling faintly. I sensed a vulnerability about her then that I would not violate.

"I've heard," I said hesitantly, "that you conduct a discussion group in your quarters by invitation only. May I become a part of this group?"

Her face lit up; she was indeed a remarkable beauty. "I'm pleased," she said, "but I warn you. The subject matter is delicate. Not everyone is ready to handle the nature of what we discuss. It can be easily misunderstood."

"I think I can manage; I'm sure I can."

She paused, studying my face before she spoke. "All right. We are discussing the topic The Girl-Nun in the Church," she said. "Are you sure you're ready? I want mature Sisters, open and with thick hides." I felt embarrassed. My youthful appearance must have given her the impression I was terribly young.

The Girl-Nun in the Church reverberated in my mind. It angered me without my knowing what it was all about. I headed toward Juliette's dormitory. The small room was crowded to overflowing. Juliette sat calm and gurulike on a yellow pillow in the center of the room. Most of the nuns present were in modified dress. Many of their Rules were in the process of change; they were visiting their families and living in convents without official Superiors. Silence was eased in favor of charity and friendship.

"Do any of you find the subject girl-nun offensive?" Juliette began.

An albino blond nun, rather plain looking, spoke up. "I do. Because it is the true description of many of us." The nuns clapped. "It describes a captive child in an ignorant body."

"Don't stop there," Juliette encouraged, her voice soothing yet challenging.

The nun seemed self-conscious, but she gained assurance as she went on. "I entered my Order at eighteen, accepted traditional obedience without question. What ever my Superior told me, I believed. It was always the will of God, the means to make me holy, a saint. I've been dependent. I can't even think for myself." She faltered, then cleared her throat. "Deep inside I feel like a little girl—emotionally, I mean. Sometimes I'm confused. Sometimes I'm in a rage . . . obedience . . . the whole thing is so unfair . . . unreal." There were tears in her eyes. The room was still, the only sound the blond nun's sobs. Her words and tears had worked their way into our hearts.

When the long silence had become almost intolerable and the nun's tears had waned, Juliette spoke again. "My dear Sisters, how many of us feel just as this Sister does?"

I glanced around the room. Every Sister was nodding.

Juliette took us all in at a glance. "Sisters, Sisters, if we are to take our place as leaders, we must grow up. We must be mature, thinking women and put away the toys of little girlhood. We should not need 'daddies' or 'mommies' to give us assurance, protection. Give up this so-called good-nun complex; put it to rest, to psychic death, forever."

There was no escaping her all-encompassing gaze. "Now," she said finally, "break into small discussion groups."

I had assumed I was ready for this, but I wasn't. The groups were knitting themselves together; Juliette moved among us. I felt on the verge of panic. One middle-aged nun smiled at me reassuringly. "This must be frightening for you," she said. I nodded.

I listened to the discussion of maturity, personal freedom, the questioning of what was really the will of God. A scholarly looking nun giggled next to my shoulder. "You know, we were never supposed to think for ourselves." Other Sisters nodded in agreement.

Then the spokesman for our group, a plain busty nun, redirected the group. "How do we rid ourselves of this little girl-nun, of the good-nun mentality?"

A tall, thin nun spoke up strongly. "We had better start reevaluating the way we think about ourselves as women and as religious women. You know what I mean: nuns in a male-dominated Church, with no power."

I hadn't spoken yet and my mouth felt dry.

The leader turned to me. "Is there anything disturbing you?"

My eyes had grown wet, and I hated myself for my immature display of emotion. "It's just that this is so much for me."

"How old were you, my dear, when you entered?" asked an older Sister.

"Almost sixteen."

Juliette had come to our group. She seemed to sense my insecurity and laid her hand on my shoulder, massaging it gently. Her touch felt cool and soothing. "What you will begin to understand if you stay with us is that we recognize ourselves as individuals. The Church has recognized us only as Sisters in Congregations. We have filled a function. For us to pass beyond this is to radicalize the Church. I am for it."

Near the end of our courses, Margaret and I joined the rest of the Toluca Team at the Smithsonian Museum. It was a reward we gave ourselves for our six weeks of hard study.

Sister Adele gathered us together before we went in. "I've been appalled at the liberties I see the nuns taking on campus," she said coldly. "I've heard of discussion groups that attack the Church. Be careful, Sisters. Stand on your guard against the liberal left." The Sisters nodded, and Margaret looked at me from the corner of her eye.

"Can we accuse anyone of being extreme," I answered, "if we haven't been a part of their discussions?"

Adele glared at me for a moment. "What I am trying to do is warn all of us, Sister, to be very prudent. Don't be so trusting, so naïve, with all this show and tell . . . and swinging hips." Her little lecture was obviously meant mostly for me. Just before we separated, she added, "We have received a dinner invitation. Father Galliano and some friends have invited us to join them tonight." Everyone began talking like excited children. "Oh, and that means you as well, Roseann, even though you are not officially a member of his Toluca Team. He made a point of asking that you come," Adele added.

Later that evening, when we entered the dimly lit restaurant room with tall candles shimmering on lime-colored linen tablecloths, I dismissed my bad feelings toward Adele. Tall elegant wineglasses were set in front of each plate. Father Galliano and two other priests watched us as we moved into the room.

"Please, Sister Roseann, sit here." Father Galliano gestured me to his right side.

The Sisters laughed and smiled stiffly, but not the clergy, who slapped each other on the shoulders, throwing up their hands, springing their laughter off the dragon-painted walls. Then Father Galliano grew serious. "Tell me, Roseann. Have you digested enough theological inquiry here these past weeks?"

"Never enough," I said. The table grew quiet.

"Sometimes too much exposes us to the betrayers of our faith," he added. "There is reason why the Catholic Church has survived so long, Sisters, in spite of your consciousness-raising groups," he continued. He spoke to me while the other Sisters shifted uncomfortably in their chairs. "The Church, in all its tradition, will go forward only because it is unchanging."

My food stuck in my throat. I hated myself for not having the courage to speak my mind. The other priests were nodding their approval, as were the Sisters. I wanted to cry out, "Who can say whose love is greater—yours, because you are men; mine, less because I am merely a nun? Must we always submit?" But I said nothing and for the first time I really understood how much a girl-nun I was.

Margaret walked with me back to our dormitory. "Nothing gets past Father Galliano," she said thoughtfully.

"Do the walls of Catholic University tell secrets, or does he get a little help from his friends?"

She looked straight ahead.

I couldn't sleep; Father Galliano's insinuations of heterical influences and the mention of Juliette's consciousness-raising groups bothered me. I wanted the old ways. They were so secure; comforting and unchanging as St. Peter's rock. But I also wanted the new ways of inquiry, of new, modern saints and abundant change in our Holy Rule. "The girl-nun is passive. She is unquestioning and always submissive to clerical power, exercised by male-dominated priesthood." This has been stamped into the bone marrow of the Church, into the mind of every nun.

I prayed, covering my face with the blanket, trying to hold on to the last drops of freedom, of freshness, of energy that were draining from my spirit. They seemed to leave me like wisps of incense floating away into the humid night.

❦ 17 ❦

Judith was overjoyed to see us all return. We paid a short visit to the chapel, asking Our Lord's blessings on a new school year. I was anxious to get myself back into community life.

"Still in Washington, Roseann?" Judith peered at me curiously as I sat dreamily listening to the hum of the washing machine in our basement laundry room.

"Yes, and my head is filled with new ideas for working with my teachers."

"Thank God. I certainly didn't want you to return a dried-up organism." She smiled good-naturedly. While I was away I had given St. Anthony's Convent little thought and now it felt good to be back here and with Judith. She was fumbling with a small letter, her smile slowly disappearing.

"Our Syracuse Superior sent me a bit of news I know will interest you." She adjusted her veil for a moment, then announced, "Sister Ruth is in the state mental hospital there."

I sank against the porcelain washer. "Good Lord! What happened?"

"No details, actually. Just that one morning Ruth admitted herself into the hospital."

"Have the Sisters seen her?"

Judith shifted her weight uneasily. "I understand Ruth is doing fine." She had evaded my question, letting me know that no one had visited her.

"May I phone Ruth?"

"I have the feeling this isn't the best time. Wait a few days, Roseann. Perhaps by then I'll know more of what's going on."

"It's a shame," I said. "The administration can't admit Sisters are human. They break down, but they closet these poor souls like it's a sin to have emotional illness." I felt grave sadness for Ruth, who had called for help. No one, especially me, had tried to ease her pain. The knowledge of my own fallibility was not a pleasant thought. But I would phone Ruth.

We hadn't heard a word about her condition, not even through the cloister's grapevine. She had become another invisible sick Sister. Saturday morning I waited anxiously for Ruth to come to the phone, hoping she'd sound well.

"Hello, Roseann." Her voice was cheerful and much lighter than I had expected. There was an awkward pause on my end as I frantically picked and discarded appropriate conversation.

"I think of you all the time," I finally said. "How are you feeling?"

She laughed. "Fine . . . really . . . fine. I've been here three months."

"Three months! I mean, I only just heard." It was shocking that her illness had been kept a secret so long.

Apparently she didn't catch the shock in my voice. She kept talking rapidly. "You're lucky to have reached me, Roseann. I'm leaving the hospital."

"Thank God for that. Wonderful! The Sisters will welcome you back," I said, praying it would be true.

"No, no . . . I'm leaving the Congregation . . . going back home; taking a practical nursing course in Ohio."

"My Lord! Leaving?"

"Roseann, my decision wasn't made on the spur of the moment. I've given it a lot of serious thought. I'm perfectly at peace with it; it's what I want to do."

I was confounded. Ruth was leaving the Order and not a word. Was she in her "right mind" or acting out her illness?

She seemed to read my mind. "When I first admitted myself here," she said, "I honestly thought I was losing my mind, but I've discovered I was never out of my mind. It's the Congregation that is sick. I don't expect you to understand," Ruth added quietly. "This is the best way. I am in excellent health."

"I believe you. I wish you happiness and God's blessings. Write me, please." She laughed, reminding me of the way she used to sound when she first came to Albany three years ago. The phone clicked.

"Jesus help her. Help me."

A week later, a poverty-stricken statement about Ruth arrived, sandwiched with other news from Mother Cora: "Our prayers follow Sister Ruth in her decision to return to secular life." Period. No one spoke of Ruth or of the fifteen years she had lived among us, a Sister in Christ.

I counted on my fingers all the Sisters who had left, the bright intelligent novices, the professed who claimed that our modernization and renewal would never come. It worried me that I needed more than ten fingers to count.

"These times test our commitment to our vows, to the service of the Church," Mother Edmond had told me recently when I visited the Motherhouse. In her own elevated state of holiness, she held this to be the only truth. Yet she had been warned years before by Father Barrett to move forward with the Church, to have her Sisters educated, to be faithful to the original spirit of our Foundress. She had not listened.

The issues of modernization and renewal of our Holy Rule, which had caused some impatient Sisters to leave, could not be avoided much longer. Our General Chapter, the meetings to decide on the changes called for by the Vatican Councils, was scheduled to begin in three months. As it was, our Order was comparatively late in this. Many other Orders had completed their Chapters. I had seen the effects everywhere on the Catholic University campus.

Judith began enthusiastic preparation for the Chapter. "You are aware, Sisters, that our General Chapter opens soon. I don't want you to be like a bunch of ignorant deadheads. This Chapter is too important. It means our future." She smiled pleasantly. "I am recruiting experts on the Church's renewal to prepare us."

It was Judith's hope that the General Chapter movement would bring us out of the "Dark Ages," where for years we had been deprived of friendships, education, and intimacy, immersed as we were in Mother Edmond's reform, draining us of our Foundress's original life, blood, and spirit.

As time for the General Chapter approached, we voted for our delegates. I prayed I would be among them. The list of Chapter delegates was posted on our bulletin board. I moved an unsteady finger down the list of names, coming to Sister Norma and then, wonderfully, to myself. My Sisters in religion had chosen me to represent them. It was cause to celebrate and I tore through the convent looking for Judith. We could rejoice together.

I found Judith engrossed in sorting catechisms. When she turned to face me, her eyes were red. I had never seen her look like this. "What's wrong?" I asked. "You should be kicking your heels high. We're delegates."

"We?"

In my excitement I had just assumed her name had been on the list. I gabbled. "Maybe someone else's name was put on. I mean, by mistake."

"Come on, Roseann, you know the administration never makes such careless mistakes."

For the first time I could remember, Judith looked drawn. There was a weariness that made her seem ages old. "Why?" I cried.

She leaned heavily against the table. "Rumor has it that

my ambition in holding Chapter renewal seminars is to make myself the next Mother General." She looked away and tears streaked down her puffy cheeks. What a terrible and cruel injustice this was. Guileless and nonpolitical Judith, to whom the Chapter meant only the instrument for much-needed reform, was to be denied participation.

I wanted to touch her, but I felt she wouldn't allow this small gesture of human comfort, something she had always given to me so generously. There was nothing I could do but suffer silently with her.

Judith called Norma and me to her office. "Although we haven't talked about it, I know how hard you have been working on preparations for the General Chapter. I think both of you can use a break. Would you like to come with me to Ronston? The parish is giving the Sisters a special collection. Mother General suggested some old-time faces might stir the parishioners to respond generously."

It had been eight years since I had left Ronston, and the prospect of seeing Father Dweyer, perhaps even Jerome, was an opportunity I didn't want to miss.

We left early Sunday morning and drove through lush countryside. It was restful and quiet. Judith looked more contented than she had in days. She parked under a shade tree behind the new high school joining the grammar school, next to the new church and the teaching Sisters' convent. Undoubtedly, Father Dweyer's accomplishments were impressive. I picked up a church bulletin. Children I had taught were announcing their marriages, some having their babies baptized. The movement of time hit me squarely. I was older.

As we walked along chatting amiably, Judith moved into the crowd and I turned around to gaze at a white-haired, blue-eyed, and still strikingly handsome man. I was suddenly gasping for air from the excitement of seeing Father Dweyer. He seemed so much like Jerome—when he was

Brother Jerome—in that moment, that certain look to his eyes.

"Father Dweyer," I called out. "Remember me?"

He looked, then looked again, and twisted his hands. I could see he was searching his mind for who I could be. When he looked back, it was as if I were a stranger. "I don't think so. Were you someone to me before the fall?"

"I am Sister Roseann," I said calmly. "Can we walk?" Gently, I placed my hand through his arm, hugging him to my side. There was a familiar warmth to the touch of his priestly black serge, immaculately pressed. "I look a little different. It's been a while," I excused.

He continued to study me. "Is there something we did together once? Was it . . . no, it couldn't be . . . Rome? Were you there for the convocation? Oh, the red hats, tossed in the air with abundant joy." He broke out laughing, throwing back his head, looking for a moment like a young man again. "And how are you doing, Sister . . . Sister . . . uh . . ."

"Roseann. I'm Sister Roseann, Father Dweyer." He reached his hand toward me. I took it, trying to hold back my tears, turning my face from his.

"Ah, tears are good for the body, good for the soul. I weep all the time, you know. It's been a long time since your dear brother died, Sister Roseann, but . . ."

My brother? I had no brother, but Father Dweyer had placed me somewhere among the many others who had come and gone in his life. I wiped my eyes and turned to him. "Yes, it was a great loss, Father. And there is something about walking this cloistered hall with so spiritual a Titan as you are that reminds me of my loss."

During Holy Mass all I saw, all I could think about, was my once beautiful idol Father Dweyer, a man once bouncing with sharpness, the Bishop's golden boy. "He burned two ends of the candle," Judith told us afterward. For what? To spend his final days a psychological invalid?

During lunch, the Sisters rejoiced over the collection

plates that had provided them with five thousand dollars, no doubt inspired by the appearance of Sisters in numbers. This should have been a wonderful time to share with my Sisters, to talk over old times, but I could hardly open my mouth.

Norma, understanding, touched my hand and whispered, "Father Dweyer is at peace; he is happy as he is and you must try to accept that fact." Of course she was right, I told myself.

When I phoned Jean, it was a light moment to hear her sound so happy. "Jerome is teaching at a private school in Buffalo, and he's in love, getting married this month."

"Thank God," I said, thinking of the strange paradox of his illness, his healing, his wanting to be everything that Father Dweyer had been. Now Father Dweyer was in a state similar to that which Jerome had left. "Dr. Ortiz spoke often of you," Jean added. "Very fondly, in fact."

"I wish he were not so far away," I found myself saying. "He was a good friend." I was anxious for the day to be done and to leave Ronston.

At next morning's Holy Mass, I kept seeing Father Dweyer's face. Why was it so hard for me to accept God's will for him? At the Prayer of the Confiteor, when I came to the words "Mea culpa, through my fault, mea maxima culpa, through my most grievous fault," I struck my breast with angry vigor, recalling my sins. I nearly cried out as a sharp pain stabbed instantly at my left breast.

Hours later, at my first private moment, I disrobed and peered awkwardly into my small bedroom mirror, wanting to know, but still shamed at having to see my breasts. There was some pinkness beside the nipple. I pressed the spot gently and found it tender to my touch. Had I struck myself so hard? The more I thought about it, the more sense it made. It will go away quickly enough, I told myself.

❦ 18 ❦

I had only a few weeks to recruit more teachers for my re-lease-time religious instruction program. It was not unlike Jesus recruiting His disciples, I mused as I drove up to John Adams School to visit the principal, Frank McClosky. He had been very supportive over the past three years and I didn't anticipate any problems this year. As I moved through the school building, I followed the familiar aroma of Mr. McClosky's pipe and it led me to the cafeteria.

He stood by a long dining room table. His middle was wider since summer. "Good to see your sweet face," he said. "Are you up for another year with our electric eels?" He managed a half grin.

"Ah, the children haven't been much trouble—most of the time." I handed him my list of teachers and the release-time schedules.

"Well, we're in for trouble this year." He tapped the stem of his pipe against a tooth, then twisted the tension kinks out of his neck.

"How so?"

"We are going to have blacks from Ellis School being bused in. I'm not worried about my faculty; my teachers are pretty open-minded." He shook his head. "But parents can cause a lot of trouble. God knows I don't want a race war." He walked toward a window. This has always been a peaceful place."

"But nothing's changed yet," I said. My efforts to console him went unnoticed.

"It's been really grim at some of the other schools," he added, his voice growing heavier.

"Listen," I said. "We can develop a program that encourages both black and white parents to work together, communicate for the best interest of their children. Why wait for trouble? We can do something positive before things get out of hand. It's worth looking into, at least," I added.

Frank McClosky laughed. "Like your fire. But you better work on God, Sister. That's all I can say."

And that's what I did for the rest of the week. Waiting for violence to erupt was sheer madness of the worst kind. The only answer was to make the situation work for everyone's best interests. I found myself knocking impatiently at Judith's office.

She looked up. "Please sit, Roseann. You tower so." She listened to my proposal.

"I think an educational seminar that would engage both black and white parents is the answer to communication. We could call it Ensuring Our Children's Futures. Better parents work together to solve problems than to fight it out on the streets. Of course I would need the cooperation of black leaders, the professionals, some mental health personnel. I don't think Frank McClosky would object. He's worried, and . . ."

"Slow down," Judith soothed. "You're taking on too much," she said. "You are giving the teacher training course, you're a delegate for the General Chapter, and now you want to start an interracial program. I fear you're spreading yourself too thin."

"But I'm not. This work has to be done," I said. "I'm not just talking about commitment to God's precepts. I live here.

We live here. This is our place on the planet and I'm frightened that it may not be safe for us."

"Well, we need the pastor's consent for you to involve yourself with this program at John Adams. That might pose a problem."

"I pray not."

She smiled, fingering her beads thoughtfully. "We'll see. The Motherhouse will not be overjoyed." I rose quickly. "Certainly, Roseann, you're aware that when anything arouses public attention, pastors, the laity, the administration might prevent this sort of initiative. It's a dangerous program these days. I must warn you of that."

"But it's the way of Christ!" I said. "Where are the leaders in our Church? The Bishops? The Mother General?"

"Calm yourself. I'm *for* you, but I am warning you—preparing you that your project will be no crown of roses."

I said nothing. She rose and continued. "A word to the wise. Keep a low profile about this at recreation. Be prudent. Save yourself some heartache." She touched me lightly on the shoulder, allowing her hand to slide down my arm to a place near my breast. The contact ordinarily would have been comforting, but I felt an urgent sensitivity, almost pain, at the pressure of her touch.

When I left Judith, I was tempted to regard her reaction as overly protective, maybe even a bit of sour grapes for not being elected a delegate to the General Chapter.

In the days following, as I recruited teachers and planned for their six-week training course, I also pondered my next move for the John Adams School project. My fear that black children would be bused into a climate of hostility intensified. Without the support of community leaders, the entire project could fail. By Friday I had a note pad filled with names of people I had never met. Perhaps Judith was right about my taking on more projects than I could handle, taking on trouble, but if that was the case, I'd find out for myself.

Monday, as soon as I stepped out of bed, I felt my breast

gingerly. It seemed to feel even more tender. Still, I was trying to convince myself I was exaggerating the whole matter. I could hardly bear the thought of having some strange doctor in New Haven examine me. The only doctor I knew was Dr. Greco and he was miles away, in Albany.

I decided that I should talk to Judith, but not about the spot on my breast. For several months I had had a slight but persistent cough, and I had a few other minor medical problems. That should be reason enough.

Later that morning, I found Judith alone in her office. "I know it's not in keeping with my vow of poverty to travel so far for a medical appointment, but I would like to see Dr. Greco. I know the administration would never approve."

Judith's eyes sparked at the mention of administration. "Naturally," she said sharply, "they wouldn't approve. Make your appointment with Dr. Greco if it gives you peace of mind."

Although I had not intended it, I was apparently indirectly benefiting from Judith's continued hurt and anger at the politics from the Motherhouse that had denied her participation in the General Chapter. I plunged into a heavy week's work on my John Adams School project and my newly made Friday appointment with Dr. Greco seemed a long way away.

I sat with Frank McClosky in his office. He studied me quietly, sucking thoughtfully on the end of his pipe while I shared my ideas about the parent's seminar "Ensuring Our Children's Futures."

"I like it. I really do," he said. "But getting the right people, the right volunteers and professionals, is a bigger than life job. It's bad enough when we pay the professionals, and as for the black community? Lord, it's going to take a lot of . . . a lot of . . ." he broke off miserably.

"Mr. McClosky, let's worry next week. Now, how do I get to Ellis School from here?"

He raised his eyebrows. "Guess you *are* serious."

I drove to Ellis School, where only blacks walked the streets. John Evans, the principal, eyed me suspiciously; his dark Afro glistened. "Can't imagine a nun wanting to help us with our communication problem, our busing problems!" Evans kicked at his desk leg.

"What I mean is, it's everyone's problem. If we don't at least try to prevent problems, the John Adams community could erupt."

Evans locked his arms across his chest and pressed his lips downward. "A really noble idea, so terribly Catholic of you. What do you know about black folks? What do you care?" He stood then, fully six-four, and impatiently gestured me to the door. "I suggest you spend the morning with us, meet the teachers, talk to the children, get to know the parents, see if this program of yours fits. I'll tell you something else. It's going to be your white folks who'll nail you to the cross, not us blacks."

Out in the hall, three first-graders ran up to me. One pulled at my rosary and asked, "What's you?"

"I am a Sister, a Catholic Sister." They looked bewildered. "I teach children about Jesus." They giggled and ran back down the hall.

They had asked what I was, not who I was. It startled me as much as Evans's reaction. I spent the morning speaking to children, to parents, and to teachers, and I was convinced they wanted the best for the children. "I don't want my child to grow up feeling he's a nobody," a young mother told me.

When I stopped back at Evans's office, I was convinced the program could work if I had the right staff to work with me. "A black psychiatrist would be wonderful."

Evans nodded his head kindly and managed a smile as he handed me a card. It read: Dr. Ernest Jones, psychiatrist, Director of Family Services. "Contact him. Tell him I sent you. He's the best around. If he is interested in the program, you then can surely thank God." When he stood to shake my hand, he added, "I also suggest you attend our PTA meetings. Let the parents get to know you, to trust you. Believe me, it will help."

Certainly this Dr. Jones would be easy to persuade, a psy-

chiatrist, director of a mental health clinic. When I stepped
into his office, I anticipated a kindly, understanding doctor.
Through his office door I heard a deep, rich voice. His attractive secretary glanced at me from time to time. I leafed
through *Ebony* magazine, through psychological journals,
and imagined myself walking across a university campus
with hardcover textbooks in my arms.

Finally the secretary opened his office door. "Dr. Jones
will see you now." Once in his room, I was struck by a wall
filled with black art surrounding a central painting, a four-
by-four-foot canvas of a black woman holding her naked
boy-child affectionately. They were so alive, I could touch
their silky skin. African sculpture was displayed on oak ped-
estals, the side wall lined with Dr. Jones's degrees and nu-
merous certifications.

Dr. Jones did not stand. "Exactly what is it you want?" His
voice bristled with animosity. Taken off guard, I fumbled for
the right words; time ticked by. "I don't have all day to wait
for you to collect yourself."

Heat rose from my back. I was enraged at his rudeness
and angry at myself for being so intimidated. "Perhaps Mr.
Evans spoke to you about the program I am proposing. Mr.
Evans spoke highly of you," I said with extreme effort.

"So?" he said.

"My intention, through this program, is to prevent racial
tension through a program of communication in the best interests of black and white children. I mean to get it started
before hostility gets out of control."

Dr. Jones sneered. "So you white religious folks need us
niggers now. You never needed us in the past, not the high
and mighty Catholic Church. You never gave a damn about
poor blacks. Never!" His voice was measured and calculat-
ing, and his eyes had narrowed dangerously.

My knees shook. Was I to be his scapegoat?

"Tell me, Sister. How many black priests do you know in
the Catholic Church?"

"None."

"Nuns?"

"One. There aren't many, Dr. Jones." I could feel the intensity of anger.

"So it's time to get on the political bandwagon; follow the dream of Martin Luther King. Right, Sister?"

"Perhaps."

"No, no, no perhaps. It's yes! You don't care about black people. The Church cares less. What you all care about is losing face. You're afraid of what us niggers are going to do. You know that! Twenty years from now, no one will care. It will be business as usual, racial hate. Nothing changes, woman. You have gall to stand here and tell me what you think black people need."

By now I was furious. "I'm telling you," I shouted, "I didn't come here to take your abuse, your outrageous disrespect. Your attitude is poison, Dr. Jones. I've regarded you as a professional. I am a nun, yes, a white woman, if you can swallow that." I was gasping for air. "You have ungodly nerve, Dr. Jones."

He stared at me like a cobra. He was very aware how he had treated me, and it was deliberate.

My hand was on his office door when I turned to face him. "I don't need the likes of you, Dr. Jones."

His mocking voice followed me. "But you do need me, Sister. You won't find anyone else in this town able to help you out. I'm talking about black power. I'm talking about influence. I have all of that. You better understand."

"You're arrogant, you're insulting, you're insensitive, Dr. Jones, a discredit to your profession, to black people."

"Get out, woman. Get out of here fast." I did.

Early the following morning when I dragged myself out of bed, Doctor Jones's angry eyes followed me to chapel. Praying for him, I felt, was like praying for the devil. I'd tell Evans what I thought about his revered doctor.

Evans listened to me. There was a long unsettling silence before he said, "The man did you a favor, Sister."

"A what?"

"I said a favor. You better grow some tough skin, lady, if you plan to run this so-called interracial program." Instantly, my thoughts returned to Sister Juliette, to the girl-nun image, to the courage that separated girls from women. But it was little consolation.

If I wanted Dr. Jones, I was going to have to reverse my attitude. The phone felt slippery in my clammy palms. "Dr. Jones," I began, forcing my voice to remain steady, "it's vital that I have you on my staff." And cost what it may to my pride, I added, "I have learned much from your honesty. I realize I still have a lot to learn, but you are the right person for this program." At first, he said nothing. I could feel the familiar roll of heat begin to move through my body.

"So you still want my services?"

"That's right. I do." There was a significant pause.

"On the condition that I take my own staff with me, that I run the program. We'll work with McClosky's counselors, but I run it my way. Understand?" I panicked for a moment. Mr. McClosky was prepared to be in charge, but Jones wasn't about to compromise. I had to take the chance.

"Fine, no problem." I prayed Mr. McClosky would agree.

"Write me a formal letter of request, Sister. Outline in detail the entire seminar program. I'll review it with my staff. Good day."

Judith took pride in my work every time I brought her up to date, and in keeping with her advice, I mentioned only censored bits and pieces of the John Adams project to the Sisters during recreation. Still, Judith had not spoken to the pastor and my anxiety grew, compounded by my fear of the spot on my breast.

Mr. McClosky was surprisingly willing to cooperate with Dr. Jones in the program, and I had the impression that it might be because it took some of the heat off him if the program failed. Mr. McClosky gave me the name of an influential contractor, Joe Lazano, to start my contacts with the Italian community. "He knows everybody and we need all the help we can get." I agreed.

* * *

I walked slowly into an expensive men's club. Joe Lazano had suggested it because it was conveniently near his home. The lobby was dimly lit. Cigarette smoke hung like a suffocating curtain and men passing by stopped to stare at me. Joe Lazano was a bull of a man, having earned his position as land developer and construction contractor by coming up from the ranks.

"Sister, are you sure you feel comfortable here?" Lazano asked, taking me by the arm, suggesting we move out of the male-dominated atmosphere. "We never have nuns visit us, not even women as pretty as you."

"I bet you say that to all the ladies you meet, Mr. Lazano," I said, picking up his spirit of conviviality.

"With care, I'd say. But you have a certain look I didn't think the Church advertises."

I felt a spread of pink cover my face. Then I launched into my prepared speech, aware that he looked at me in a way that made me still feel uncomfortable yet oddly excited.

"You must be aware that with the plan to bus black children from Ellis School, we are already experiencing communication problems, tension."

"You mean racial hatred, don't you, Sister?" he interrupted. "You're much too nice."

"All of that."

"Let's go somewhere more quiet. Guiseppe," he called out suddenly. A slight, old man came hurrying up. "The Sister and I will have lunch." I took a slight step backward, thinking of our Order's Rule, which would forbid it.

He had lapsed temporarily into Italian, but now he spoke to me. "Guiseppe is from Naples; I'm from Sicily. We speak dialects that are probably as old as the language of the Church."

I followed Mr. Lazano; I had decided that I would risk the Rule. He led me to a table in a high ceilinged, oak-paneled dining room filled with wonderful smells that reminded me of my hunger.

"Now, Sister Roseann, you're going to tell me you have a vision that will allow us parents to work in the best interest of our children."

I laughed. "Ensuring our children's futures," I said quickly. "You have children in our school."

"So I'm a likely choice?"

"Yes. Of course, there's to be more involved," I hurried to add. He sat back in his chair as I continued. "I don't want just the typical involvement of PTA mothers. We need concerned fathers."

"Like Joe Lazano."

"Exactly."

"Doesn't it bother you that I'm not a dyed-in-the-wool Catholic?"

"I think your concern for your children is not inconsistent with the concern of the Church."

"In that respect, you have a point. Then, I have pull in the community. So you think that makes me a community leader? I don't get it, Sister. Do you want power or do you want good Catholics?"

"Both, if I can get them. You seem rather hostile," I replied.

"It's a sore point with me, the power of the Catholic Church, what it teaches. Has been for years."

"Regardless of what you believe, I need you for this program."

"I believe you mean it, but are we talking about my energy, my time, or my personal finances? What do you have in mind, Sister?"

"All of that."

Later as we walked out of the club, he suddenly pointed down the street to where a dark-haired child played. "That's my home. Take a look at Justine. She's my honey-bear." His voice softened wonderfully. I stopped, shaken by the sight of something else. Parked in front of his house was a familiar truck with bold block letters on the side door: JONATHAN RANDALL, CONTRACTOR.

I forced myself to sound calm. "Do you have other contractors working for you?"

"Have for years. Subcontract a lot of my work. That truck belongs to an old friend. He's doing a job here, spending the weekend with me. Say, come on over. He'll take to you. I know his taste."

"No . . . no . . ."

"Okay. Tell you what. Phone me Monday. I'll let you know if I can be of any help." He smiled warmly and waved.

Jesus, help me. Jonathan! I nearly ran back to my car for fear he would step out of the house. Lord, let Joe Lazano forget to mention me to him, please!

❦ 19 ❦

The drive to Dr. Greco's office in Albany was a tug-of-war of anxieties among Jonathan's strange reappearance, the John Adams project, the teacher training course, and my preparation for the General Chapter. Now there was this strange pinkness beside my left nipple and the more recent appearance of a tiny lump.

By the time Dr. Greco's nurse ushered me into the small examining room, I felt near collapse. "Please undress," the nurse directed with a practiced smile and cool detachment. A white gown covered my tense body, but not the layer of terror twisting inside me.

My eyes fastened on the door, both dreading it to open and wanting it to. There was a gentle knock preceding Dr. Greco's smiling countenance.

"Thank you for seeing me," I said. "I understand your practice has grown so much you haven't been taking on new patients." Although I had not been his patient, I had met him when accompanying other nuns who were.

He scanned his clipboard carefully. "When was the last time you had a complete medical examination, Sister?"

"When I was fifteen, just before I entered the convent."

"I'll never understand the backward practices of so many

religious orders. Yours is the worst." His voice rose. "I'm not angry with you, but I see disease every day, eating ripe, beautiful bodies of too many women of God because of ignorance, willful ignorance. But you're here, and I intend to give you my best." He smiled slightly.

"Please relax. Your heart is pounding as if you've run a marathon." He held my hand for a moment, giving me assurance. The healing energy of doctors, I thought, remembering Dr. Ortiz.

"Have you ever had a pap smear?"

"No." I didn't even know what it was.

"Have you ever had your breasts examined?"

I shook my head, pinching my eyes shut.

"It's a rather simple exam if you don't knot yourself up, as you're doing this moment. Take some deep breaths. Before you know it, the exam will be over." The door opened and his nurse came in to assist him.

She put a small pillow under my head, adjusting my feet on the stirrups, uncovering my legs to the edge of my kneecaps. I felt the color rush to my face. She helped him put on his rubber gloves. Every muscle in my lower extremities was cramping. How dare he invade my body! How dare he touch my sacred virginal sanctuary! I struggled not to cry.

"Sister, at the worst this will be mildly uncomfortable. It won't hurt," he said firmly. "Please try to relax. Otherwise you're creating the pain." I bit my lips, trying to breath in controlled measures, but my body held rigid. Dr. Greco sighed and began to proceed in spite of my resistance, reaching in sideways, where he inserted the speculum slowly and gently, pressing with one finger on the bottom wall of my vagina to guide the cold instrument in. I felt a cut and twitched uncontrollably; then his rubber gloves withdrew expertly. The stretched fullness subsided, but my mind had frozen in the abyss of this humiliation. Dr. Greco had touched something that was meant to be untouchable. I couldn't look at him.

He started to press down on my stomach, slowly working up, asking, "Pain, Sister?"

"No," I answered, until he had reached my right breast. His fingers pressed gently. I would not allow myself to admit the slightest pleasure, not even the sensation of my hardened nipple. He moved to my left breast, repeating the same circular ritual, then used a magnifying glass. I wanted it all to end, end now. He could see that I was crying, but in his own understanding, he said nothing.

"Well, the first round is over with," he announced. "My nurse will take you to the lab for a blood sample and urinalysis. When you're finished, I'll see you back in my office." He left me with the nurse.

I tried to stand; my legs gave way. I laughed nervously. My gown was drenched. Had he found anything? I prayed, superstitiously bargaining with God, bribing Him with promises I could never keep.

The abundant sunlight in Dr. Greco's office gave his green plants the look of radiant good health, a welcome contrast to the sterile white examining room.

"Please sit." He gestured toward a chair, his voice exceptionally cheerful as he thumbed through my chart.

Then I blurted out, "Am I all right? Is anything wrong?"

He laughed heartily. Apparently this same question had been put to him, in just such a manner, thousands of times. "Sit back in your chair, Sister. The world hasn't come to an end with one examination." At least the leather chair supported my twitching body.

"You'll get the lab test results in ten days, but regarding your left breast"—he paused for a second—"there is definitely a pinkness, a very, very slight formation of a swelling, a lump, perhaps."

"A lump?" I felt as if I were being crushed, that I wouldn't be able to lift my body from the chair. I hung my head.

"Come now, Sister. Worry is the refuge of masochists," he cautioned. "I've had women come in here with the same symptoms, believe me, and it's been nothing, nothing."

I studied his eyes for deception. Was he being honest or pacifying a desperate woman? How many women end up with breast cancer?

"My nurse will set up your next appointment, but you *must* examine your breast in the manner I showed you. Understand?"

"Yes."

As if reading my mind, he added, "There is nothing sinful, nothing wrong in doing this, Sister. The pap smear hasn't made you any less in the eyes of God." No doubt he had dealt with many nuns. Thank God for that.

Judith absorbed the details of my medical account matter-of-factly, though the mention of my breast with its pinkness brought a tingle of color to the tip of her nose. "I wouldn't worry," she said, watching me twist my rosary beads into tortured knots. "Follow Greco's advice; see him in two weeks. Worry is the devil's workshop, my dear."

In chapel, I tried to put myself together. Here I was in an absolute state of panic. This was one more opportunity sent from God to test me, to work through fear. I gave myself a stronger pep talk during evening prayer, where I was still shaky, but more hopeful.

I resolved not to look at my breast, not even to touch it, not to think about it or waste my mind worrying. And this resolve of denial gave me comfort. Besides, I had more projects going than I ever had in my entire religious life to absorb my attention. Thank God!

♥ 20 ♥

Monday morning I called Joe Lazano's office. Again, I prayed that he had not told Jonathan about me. "Have you come to a decision?" I asked, coming directly to the point.

"I have. It will be costly in some respects—my time, and you get nowhere without putting cash into a program. Believe me, I know. But I'll give it a decent try."

"Wonderful! Bless you! Wonderful!" I shouted.

"Easy does it, Sister. Said give it a try, not conversion," he chuckled.

"That's all I ask." I gave him the meeting schedule and he gave me a list of likely candidates to support the program, anticipating what I had intended to ask. He never mentioned Jonathan's name; probably forgot the whole incident, I thought confidently. I liked Joe; I sensed that he was an opportunist, as I was. He liked power, as I did. Through this experience I was beginning to understand and admit such feelings.

The following evening, I attended my first PTA meeting at Ellis School. I was terribly self-conscious of my white skin among all those black faces, of being onstage as a white Catholic nun.

*   *   *

When I gave Judith a detailed account of my progress, she rubbed her fingers thoughtfully over her round chin. "I've been thinking these past weeks. Do share your progress, your insights, with the Sisters. Otherwise we would be hiding your shining light under a bushel basket. God knows we need enlightenment."

"What if the pastor doesn't approve, or the Motherhouse?" I asked.

"If we spend our lives seeking approval, ignoring the graces within our souls, great things would never be accomplished." Her lower lip quivered slightly. I detected rebellion in her tone; something that had taken the place of the fervor she had formerly spent for the General Chapter before they had rejected her. The pain and anger were still with her.

By the end of the week, all my contacts for the school project had been made.

Frank McClosky worried aloud. "Just hope the parents show," he said, pulling at his pipe.

"We have Joe Lazano, Browncoft, Whitehead. Your illustrous PTA parents will flock in just out of curiosity."

He laughed. "Right you are. Well, Tuesday will test the waters."

I couldn't allow myself other than faith at this point. Too much was happening. And for the next few days I had to be free to concentrate on the first meeting of the General Chapter.

I was deeply aware of how important the outcomes from the Chapter could be to the future of our Order. If our Sisters were going to make a difference, a real difference, in the world, we would have to move in the direction of many of the nuns I had met at Catholic University. I thought of Judith. She certainly was not a radical reformer, but her relaxed application of the Holy Rule had given a quality to our lives, a vitality to our work, that was missing in many of our other convents.

Sister Norma and I drove to the Motherhouse, picking up Sister Michele en route.

"Do you like Syracuse?" I asked. I watched her as much as I listened to her answer. Michele was our Order's only black Sister, and she was a pleasure to see. There was a sensuousness about her features, faintly suggesting the exotic. The warm brown tone of her skin was enhanced by the extreme contrast between the blackness and whiteness of her habit.

She was saying, ". . . best place I've ever lived. I'm getting fat with all the pasta the parishioners bring." She lightened my mood. Her race apparently had not posed a problem at St. Lucy's, where she was Superior.

For the remainder of the trip we planned strategy for the Chapter. Very recently Mother Cora had stepped down because of poor health, and the crown of power had passed on once again, this time to Sister Henry, who was now Mother General and more regal than ever. Mothers Edmond and Cora, of course, continued to serve in her administration. Thinking about this, I suddenly realized why my otherwise nonpolitical Judith was such a threat to them. If she were to reach the Mother Generalship, she could not be depended upon to preserve the old network. For just a moment I felt nauseated.

"The conservatives will be led by Mother Edmond," Michele said.

"Who do we have?" I asked.

"The problem is we don't have enough liberals, I fear, to balance out the Chapter," Norma said.

"Maybe less, but we might have a slight edge," Michele offered thoughtfully.

"Better be significant," Norma said.

"We're better prepared," Michele answered.

"You have a point," I added, "but Mother Edmond is tough as nails. She stands for the community's conservative reform in the 1950s. She is the rock of tradition, and it isn't change or innovation she'll fight for." It grew silent in the car.

"We'll know where everyone stands soon enough, Sisters," Norma announced as she drove up the dirt road to the

Motherhouse, past lines of cars parked by guest cottages. The atmosphere rippled with excitement and anticipation. This solemn meeting in response to the Church's renewal was the most serious event since the founding of our Order.

Prior to the opening session of the Chapter, small groups of Sisters huddled tightly together, their heads lowered like those of football players plotting their moves. The chapel bell pealed the song of the Angelus, echoing for miles into the distant resort village of Clover. As the Sisters moved into the Motherhouse's foyer, a haze of silence descended on us all. It was the moment I thought would never come when I had walked the halls of Catholic University, when I had listened to Sister Juliette. Had it come too late? Would it really change deep-seated attitudes or just be a Band-Aid dressing to wounds that had festered for decades?

"Come, Holy Spirit, enlighten our minds, open our hearts to your inspiration," prayed Mother Henry, standing majestically before us.

The Sisters sat at a round table, everyone's behavior open to the smallest nuance of detection.

Mother Henry remained standing. "As you each know, we have been chosen to represent our Sisters, their hopes, their desires, as we move forward with Holy Mother Church in the revision of our Holy Rule. Change will be achieved only through a consensus of votes, only after profound discussion and reflection on each topic. We must rise above personal preference and seek the will of God for the progress and renewal of Social Work Sisters of Immaculate Mary."

Boldly, I looked around. Mother Edmond's head was prudently bowed. I looked over to Sister Janice, branded a liberal. She gave me a knowing wink.

The hottest issue this first weekend was the modernization of our religious habits.

Mother Edmond spoke first. "Our religious habit gives witness to the world that we belong to God. It is the outward manifestation of our commitment; even the armed services insist their members be noticed for what they stand for. How much more we, in the service of the Church." She arched her back, lifting her chin. Nothing had changed in her. She looked older, though she showed few wrinkles. Her beauty was still breathtaking. It had been years now since I had given up the notion of being like her, the dream of most bright-eyed novices, but I loved her nonetheless. She had not broken as had Father Dweyer, Ruth, Martha, and so many more.

We were each allotted ten minutes to air our views before the final vote was taken.

I raised my hand. Mother Henry acknowledged me with what seemed to be a hint of warning on her face.

"Regarding the holy habit, Sisters." I looked around the table. Each face was familiar, including the tight-jawed Maurice. Some looked at me and I sensed distrust. What dare I say after Mother Edmond had spoken. But others looked at me with hope.

"Sisters," I began again, "the religious habit was originally meant to be identified with the common dress of the people. Christ didn't make a spectacle of himself by what He wore; even our Foundress insisted we wear secular garb in the 1920s. Our personal commitment isn't less holy because we don't wear black or veils or long skirts. Children ask *what are we?* Therefore, my Sisters in Christ, I propose, in accordance with the Church's urgings, we return to secular dress . . ."

I had barely sat down when fifteen hands shot wildly in the air. Some angry looks were sent in my direction, but Mother Henry remained expressionless. The debate grew hotter for the remainder of the weekend. "It's crazy and senseless, this fighting about what we must wear," I complained to Norma and Michele. "We should be discussing how to get educated, how to become friends, what silence means when it is filled with love, not tension or fear of our Superiors' disapproval." I was exhausted from the sheer pettiness of it all, from the diehards, and I wondered if I had made any worthwhile contributions besides arousing disapproval.

"We'll be joining the war zone every weekend for some time to come," Michele smiled when I complained.

I laughed at myself, at how much I had wanted to be a part of this Chapter.

When we returned to the convent, Judith handed me a letter from Dr. Ortiz. Actually, there was no letter, just a photo of him with a small group of brown children in front of a clinic. On the back it read: "Witch Doctor Brujo . . . Ignacio Ortiz." I dreamed peacefully of him that night. If only he had not left me. I needed his wisdom, his understanding, his touch, his healing.

I woke in the middle of the night and peered cautiously at my breast. Cooperate with Dr. Greco? I must, I thought as I lay back on the pillow, tossing and turning, pulling the covers over my head. But then again I rationalized: You'll be asking for trouble. The old slogan out of sight, out of mind gave me an odd sense of reassurance and once more I found myself willing to hide my breast.

The next day, I thought it the proper time to invite the Sisters to attend the John Adams project seminar after dinner. "Your presence this evening will encourage the parents," I said. "It will show how much Catholic Sisters care for their children's futures." There was an awkward moment of silence. Margaret spoke first.

"I wish I could be with you, but the Toluca Team leaves for Danbury early tomorrow." They didn't look sorry, except for Norma.

After recreation, Judith waited for me in the dining room. "Don't be too angry at the Sisters, Roseann. They have lived in tunnels so long that leaving them and facing the light without fear will take time."

"You're putting it rather kindly," I said.

"Perhaps." The phone rang and Judith left me pondering her words. When she returned, she looked deeply concerned.

"The pastor insists you not go to the seminar, that you drop your involvement immediately. I'm sorry, Roseann. He's the boss; we work for him. Nothing I could say changed his attitude."

"You mean underneath it all he's an out-and-out racist?"

"It's more than personal feelings, I'm sure," she said.

"Don't you see what will happen if I don't show up? The whole thing will blow up, the black community will tell me they were right about the Church. Jesus help us! We can't back off now. Please, I beg you, let me go. I'll take my chances. Please!" I grabbed the car keys.

The auditorium was noisy and filling up quickly. Mr. Mc-Closky moved quickly from parent to parent in a flurry of excitement. There were as many black parents as white. Mr. Evans whispered, "Thought you were going to show up with the entire Catholic Church." I blushed. I was alone, and it hadn't gone unnoticed.

Mr. McClosky called the meeting to order. "We have come together for these seminars, fittingly named 'Ensuring Our Children's Futures,' initiated by Sister Roseann. Please stand, Sister, so everyone can see who you are." The room filled with applause. He then introduced Dr. Jones and his staff, then his own staff. The program began with Dr. Jones's bass voice ringing through the auditorium. He spoke firmly but without anger.

Parents were grouped at tables of twelve, with a staff member leading the discussion at each table. Wherever angry voices rose, in an instant Dr. Jones moved in and returned the calm. It was not an easy beginning, talking to each other, experiencing their differences face to face, but it had begun. I forced myself not to think of the consequences for me.

Dr. Jones approached me when the program was over. "A nice turnout, Sister. I have been surprised and pleased." He turned abruptly and left with his staff.

The pastor avoided me; even his curates looked past me.

The Sisters never referred to the seminar, and Judith, I knew, supported me silently, expecting the worst to happen.

I finally received my medical reports. Pap smear, blood test, urinalysis were all negative. Another appointment for my breast examination was scheduled for the following Friday. "Please confirm," the letter read. If everything else was normal, why should I worry? I asked myself.

But I rushed to my bedroom, closed the door silently, and took off my habit to peer at myself in the mirror. Handling my breast gingerly, I searched for the lump. It hadn't gotten worse. I phoned Dr. Greco's office.

The nurse, cool and amiable as ever, said, "Wait one moment, Sister."

Then Dr. Greco was on the phone. "I know you're relieved about your test results, but it's imperative I monitor your breast. Have you been feeling it, observing it regularly?"

"Yes," I lied.

"Sister, you should keep your appointment, but I can't force you."

I hesitated. Albany was so far away. I felt fine. I said nothing.

"Notify me immediately if there are any changes," he continued. "Watch for growth, for increased pinkness or pain. Feel your breast in the manner I showed you. Do you understand?"

"I do, and thank you, Doctor." The phone clicked heavily. I tried to convince myself I was doing the right thing, that I was taking pains not to indulge myself, that I wouldn't allow myself to become a hypochondriac. Besides, I was so very busy. The John Adams School project was launched and doing well. The General Chapter was under way, and now my third priority, the teacher training program, needed my attention.

❦ 21 ❦

The teacher training course, which I called "Celebration of Life," had gone well. As I was preparing for its windup, it was fortunate, in a sense, that I could not see how many of the threads that had made this a particularly busy and productive period were pulling apart.

Three of St. Anthony's Sisters came to the training program, and the convent basement was filled with seasoned volunteer teachers and inexperienced newcomers, eager to work with our public school children. As I moved to the podium, the room fell silent. In a back corner, a blue-eyed young priest with wavy black hair watched me with open, unashamed interest. He loosened his Roman collar and leaned back in his chair. It was Father Covina.

After every class he lingered until the teachers had left the convent. I looked forward to these times with him. He poked through my posters, moving close to me. The excitement I had never forgotten with Jonathan hit me again. "You're taking on a lot," he said in an easy drawl, "with this Agape Feast for your last class."

"It's fitting, don't you think? Agape, the love feast. It's what the course is all about. The teachers are enthused."

"It's rather ambitious," he said in a low enticing tone, "but you do things that provoke, that are dangerous—such as your John Adams program. Do you like to play with danger?"

I heard Judith call from the hall, "Roseann? Are you still there?"

"See you." He grinned and sauntered out the convent's back door.

Before I could turn around, Judith was beside me. "What's all this chit-chat with Covina about?"

"We always talk after class."

"You're flirting. It's outright flirting. My dear, are you really so unaware?"

I looked away. Was I such an open book? It shocked me as much as her accusation.

"Don't spend any more time with Father Covina. He's a young man, a young priest. He doesn't need distractions."

I talked to Norma. She listened kindly.

"Maybe I am flirtatious," I admitted. "But doesn't chastity get easier with age?"

Norma started to laugh. "Whoever told you it gets easier?"

"Confessors, some of them. My Novice Mistress, Superiors."

Norma, sensitive then to my hurt, grew serious. "Oh, Roseann, you're in for a sad awakening. It can get much harder, depending on the individual. After thirty, some women become more sexually aroused." Her eyes grew large. She had been a former high school counselor and had entered the Order at age thirty-five. I felt she, at least, knew what she was talking about.

"It takes courage, faith, and discipline to remain faithful to a state of chastity." She seemed sorry she had to teach me what the convent never taught. "Come now, be joyful, Roseann," she said. "You've managed so far."

Over the next few weeks, my emotional life regained its balance. Father Covina noticeably avoided me, and I knew Judith had spoken to him. I felt changed somehow toward her. I felt she had treated me like a child, and I resented it.

With a tinge of guilt and sadness, I wished I felt the same about her. We had been a group of silent women, invisible to each other, living together but isolated in a chilling, cold world. Better this pain of friendship with Judith, than the emptiness of detachment.

The "Celebration of Life" course ended with the grand Agape feast. The convent basement was filled to capacity and the setting sun colored the windows and shone on tall blue candles set in mounds of fresh-made bread. Father Galliano had accepted my invitation to participate in the final ceremony, but St. Anthony's pastor, still angry with my involvement in the John Adams project, was conspicuously absent.

The energy to which I had given myself in teaching this course, and in the interracial program felt much like the same energy I had had at the age of fifteen when I ran on the beach with my twin. Recently, I had felt more like the long-distance runner in a second wind; every effort brought me new life.

A guitarist strummed lightly, moving his fingers to the beat of the teachers' songs. Dancers moved gracefully to the choreographed celebration of life. Father Galliano lifted the Sacred Host before us. "The body of Christ," he said, and in the moment I felt the love of Jesus and His joy. This celebration must not end. It must live forever, I told myself.

Father Covina gave the kiss of peace and we hugged, even kissed each other. Music and laughter filled the hall. The love feast would be celebrated in the sharing of food. Hostesses brought out chicken, salads, roast beef, and desserts of every kind.

Father Galliano approached me during the meal, beaming. "Success is yours, I see, by the enthusiasm of your teachers."

"It's been a marvelous experience," I replied.

"Come work for me," he said.

"That's up to our Mother General." I laughed, flattered

that he wanted me for his own staff even if he might be teasing.

Judith, pink with happiness, rushed to me, kissing me unashamedly on the forehead. "You've done a wonderful job. I'm proud of you." Although she couldn't express publicly how good she felt about my involvement at John Adams, that I had gone through with it without the approval of the pastor, at least this gave her the opportunity to praise me openly.

She presented me with a gift package from my class, a hand-carved wooden statue of Our Lady of Hope. In a folder were letters, heart-moving essays on what "Celebration of Life" had meant to them.

As I was coming in from a late night meeting several days later, Judith met me at the door. "Are you aware that Father Galliano has been putting pressure on Mother Henry to get you on his Toluca Team?"

"What? I'm exhausted and . . ."

"Roseann, I asked you a question."

"Judith, may I come in? I'm also starved."

"Oh yes. I'm sorry." She closed the door gently behind me and led the way to the kitchen.

"Any leftovers?"

"I'll fix you something. Sit down." She began preparing a thick tunafish sandwich, but appeared distracted. "I petitioned Mother Henry that you be transferred to his team."

"And?"

"She refused. I tried my best, God knows."

I gulped a bite of my sandwich. "How could she? I gave one of the best training courses in years. That's what Galliano told me. I mean, look at all the courses I've taken. What reasons can she possibly give?"

Judith looked away, putting the leftover food into the refrigerator.

"Oh, God. You're holding out on me. There's something else, isn't there?"

She finally looked into my eyes and with enormous effort spoke. "Roseann, I have prayed that you won't take this badly, but . . ."

"But what?"

"Mother Henry is transferring you to St. Lucy's Convent in Syracuse, effective Tuesday. Three days . . ."

"Transferred! Transferred? Three days?"

"Come to my office, please." There, Judith dropped heavily into her chair, gesturing for me to sit. "Before you explode, listen to me."

"Listen? I'll tell *you*, Judith. I'm going to spare you the farce of polite religious words. I'll tell *you*." I was shouting.

Judith held my gaze. She had prepared herself for battle.

I went on blindly, "You know something? The administration, Henry, can't accept that one of their Sisters is getting much too much notoriety. Father Galliano wants me; no doubt our noninvolved Sisters have complained about the John Adams project. God knows what the pastor told her, and she can hardly stand me at the General Chapter. You just try to deny any of this. Deny it!" I waited for her to clear her throat, to fight me.

"Yes," she finally replied. "You're right, Roseann. Never deny the truth you feel." The thinness of her response shocked me. Hot tears ran down my cheeks.

"My God. The John Adams project couldn't be at a more critical point. What do I tell McClosky? Jones? Evans? Everybody? How can I explain? I'm *dangerous*!"

Judith shook her head. "You can't. Henry has also excused you from attending the last meeting of the Chapter this weekend."

"How thoughtful. But I *will* go."

"Fine."

"You know, Judith, I'm being punished, shamed, because I've gone forward." My voice cracked and I reached for the doorknob to support myself. "Judith, I don't believe sainthood means the Way of the Cross, not this kind. What has happened to love? To trust? That's all I've ever really wanted

for myself from my Sisters. What is so shameful, so re-
proachable, so sinful about this? It's what I am supposed *to
be about.*" The explosion sent stabbing pains through my
breast. I could hardly breathe.

Judith rose and moved her hands over my shoulders
gently. "Despite your hurt, my dear, this will pass in time."
She rubbed the back of my neck in the familiar effort to calm
me. "I won't offer you weary explanation," she said. "Be
true to your own self, whatever the cost." It was curious;
despite my anger, my sorrow, her quiet words bore into my
soul. I took my wounded self to my room.

Later that night I jumped back against the bathroom wall
when I thought I perceived greater fullness in my left breast.
The pinkness seemed the same. Gingerly, I touched my right
breast, then frantically my left. I lost control, touching from
left to right, until I was in such a frenzy I couldn't think. I
rested my naked skin against the cold porcelain sink, allowing the enamel to soothe my hot troubled body.

Calm down, Roseann, before you scare yourself to death.
Then I came to a rather clinical decision in the best interest
of living and of the work that was yet to be done. I would
check my breasts twice a week for the next two weeks as if
they were a cold instrument. At least I could be sensible
about this.

The next day was Saturday and I phased in and out of
sleep most of the day. Sunday I left my room feeling a sense
of life return to my body, but with it all, the worry I had
repressed. It frightened me that I could put myself into such
a physical condition. I dared not think of my breast, especially now, or how I'd get to see Dr. Greco. I would face
that after I got to Syracuse. Tuesday, I would be forced to
leave. There would be no face-to-face good-byes, only
quick phone calls. Jesus, what are you doing to me?

Sunday evening the Sisters were summoned to the community room to hear about the last session of the General
Chapter, which I had missed after all.

Norma sat by Judith, thumbing through a handful of

notes. She spoke strongly. "Modification of our religious habit has been approved in accordance with stated guidelines. Sisters may visit their families every three years, beginning with the senior Sisters this year. We may attend retreats other than those given at the Motherhouse. Our mail will no longer be read by Superiors. TVs are permitted, and we may eat with the laity."

The Sisters broke out in spontaneous clapping; even the conservatives seemed pleased to have the privileges. They would be gradually introduced into the convents, according to each Superior's understanding, regardless of what we had voted on. Nothing had been mentioned about encouraging friendship, though we could hug each other in greeting. Nothing was said about silence, though we had voted that charity and common sense should take its place and fill the void that had grown with abuse for years.

Norma posted the college list on the bulletin board. I closed my eyes after I reached the board, hoping when I opened them the first name would be my own. I scanned the short list. My name wasn't there, yet Sisters much my junior, Sisters who cared nothing for education, were plainly on the list. I was in a state of shock. Any physical weakness I had been experiencing retreated before my anger. I pushed past the other Sisters into Judith's office, unannounced.

"I know," she offered. "I can't understand it either. It doesn't make any sense. Regardless of your transfer, you seemed to have had everyone's support."

"*Everyone's?*" I fired back incredulously. "*Everyone's?* So where's my name?"

Judith backed off, laying a finger to her lips and the other hand gently on my arm. It was a move she used often to calm me, but I rejected it now. She said, "Don't lose faith. Sister Lisa will be here tomorrow. She's in charge of the college program." Judith paced the floor as if trying to focus a plan.

"Are you thinking," I said angrily, "I should put my case before her?"

"From now on, Roseann, you must fight for the rights you hold so dear. You have a liberal stance, but don't forget the Church is rigidly conservative. It must be to maintain control, to keep it powerful. Religious Orders follow the same tradition."

I was humiliated that I had to beg for what I deserved.

Judith added another jab. "Do you think you're above the common struggle? Do you think that fighting for your rights is beneath you?"

"But it's insulting, Judith. I'm so torn. I can think of nothing else except the fact they have not loved me enough."

And I thought of nothing else until Lisa came early Monday morning, three years after she had left in defeat from Martha's whipping. She listened as I tried to explain.

"I've been in the Congregation nineteen years; I have managed along the way to get two years of college credits. I want to get my degree. If I'm forced to wait, they may never allow me . . ."

Lisa's gaze drifted from time to time around Judith's office, no doubt recalling the pain of her leaving. She straightened her back to the chair, lifting her chin to a sharp point, reminding me of her new elevated position as Assistant Mother General. "I can't promise you anything except that I'll do my best. Of course Mother Henry and the counselors must approve." That cold reminder wasn't what I wanted to hear.

"What college are you interested in?" she asked.

"A secular college. Syracuse. I'd major in psychology. I would get scholarships."

She laughed. "Even the Sisters attending Catholic colleges don't get scholarships. Now that would be impressive. I'll let you know the administration's decision after you've arrived at St. Lucy's. I pray that God's blessings be with you." She rose, leaving me alone. Still I felt she would present my case before the administration with conviction, but I had no more illusions about the will of God. It would be the interplay of strong wills and politics at best.

When I knelt before the tabernacle in the chapel, my body, my soul, my spirit felt ages old. The joy of the General Chapter with its many hard-won victories, thanks to a well-prepared group of fighting liberals, would have, under other circumstances, given me great joy. Now I felt only numb. My thoughts moved to the many phone calls to be made.

Mr. Evans listened quietly at first. "Bit sudden, wouldn't you say? Your leaving us?"

"Sudden change is always expected in the life of a nun," I said, biting my tongue at the obvious deceit.

"I don't doubt you, Roseann," he said curtly. "It's what you would like me to believe, but please, please. The real reasons are much too plain, aren't they?"

"Oh?"

"I told you from the beginning, nuns just don't go about helping black folks without fireworks blasting off. Looks like your Church didn't care to back up your social action program." Evans paused. "What's so regrettable about the whole thing is that I expected as much. This program lasted longer than I had anticipated. Shocked the hell out of me."

I didn't answer. I didn't want him to know I was crying.

"Who's your replacement?"

"I have no replacement."

"Figures."

When I spoke again, my voice was shaky. "Thank you for your support, Mr. Evans."

"Well, then." He cleared his voice. "Good luck in your new . . ."

"Mission," I said.

He laughed. "I can tell you this now, but I didn't think you could begin to cut it. I was wrong. I'm glad."

I spoke to Frank McClosky. He was too shaken to say much, but he promised he'd carry on the program. And I detected a horrible drop in his voice when he said "promise."

Dr. Jones was away for the weekend. I hated to think what he would say when he read my letter; such a cold response to a man who had given more than I could have dreamed of. By the time I phoned Joe Lazano, my remarks were well rehearsed and I felt nothing could surprise me.

"I knew they'd pull you out, for God's sake," he answered. I could almost see him sucking his cigar. "The Church won't stand for anything too controversial. You've known that, I'm sure."

"Perhaps." All their reactions were distressingly similar. "But I don't feel guilty for trying," I offered.

"Best thing you've said, Roseann. I got tired of feeling guilty when I was nineteen; tired of feeling guilty for making love, guilty for missing Mass, for not making perfect acts of contrition, not believing in hell and what do you call it, limbo, all that nonsense. God's no policeman. I say this, Sister. Organized religion puts shackles on people's visions. It stinks. No offense, but it plain stinks to high heaven."

He had said much the same thing many times, but at that moment it was as if I was hearing him for the very first time.

"I live a good life," he continued heatedly. "I take care of my family, my kids. We're not hurting, but a lot of my friends hurt to hell, 'cause of this religion stuff. Hey, I'm going to heaven without the Catholic Church. Sounds simple doesn't it, Sister?"

"Not really."

"Odd how religion doesn't work without the threat of hell and damnation. Controls us, that's what I say. By the way, what's your new address? Folks around here might want to write."

It sounded strange repeating the address that tomorrow would become my new home.

"Incidentally, we have a mutual friend," Joe added.
"Who?"

"My friend Jonnie Randall. Says he knows you."

I sank deeper into my chair, stunned. "Jonathan!" So Joe had told him about me.

"He's working in Syracuse." Joe laughed.

I cringed at the thought that Jonathan might have told him

everything. After I hung up, a curious thing happened. The notion that Joe would give Jonathan my new address didn't intimidate me. That it didn't was not even shocking. In the midst of my turmoil, the prospect even gave me a tinge of pleasure.

Judith respected my request that the Sisters not be told of my transfer until I had left. I was protecting myself from the possibility of their indifference more than from sadness of parting. The consolation of saying good-bye to Norma, who would care, was denied me because she was away on a two-day convention. I wanted to spend more time with Judith, but every last minute was spent in putting my parish work in order for my unnamed successor.

ST. LUCY'S CONVENT
Syracuse, New York

☙ 22 ☙

At noon Tuesday, I arrived at my new home, St. Lucy's Convent, a simple, unobtrusive building nestled solidly within the comforting folds of a heavily Italian community. The convent was located three blocks from the rectory. I had become acquainted with St. Lucy's Superior, Sister Michele, during the General Chapter sessions. I had, as much as our Order would allow, a sense of being friends with her. During the hard and sometimes hot debates of the Chapter, Michele and I were on the same side of most issues and we frequently teamed effectively in making our points.

There wasn't any doubt in my mind that Sister Michele wore her Superiorship well and exercised judicious authority. At General Chapter she had told me she ran the convent in a democratic spirit, far removed from the tradition of police matron. She had read my yellowed retreat notes from Father Barrett, even taking her own notes from mine and quoting them at Chapter.

Michele greeted me with open warmth, clasping her arms tightly around me. It was permitted now, though Mother Edmond had voted against it. "I am glad you are with me," Michele said. "Come, Roseann, let me show you our convent. I love its old-fashioned coziness."

In a snug corner of the recreation room, Sisters Anthony and Marcel sat contented before the television set, which had just arrived hours before me, a gift from our pastor, Father Patanelli, one of the few pastors we worked for who couldn't wait for our Order to get on with renewal. We were now permitted radios in the convent, even in our cars; however, this was only according to the whim of the Superiors. It didn't matter what was in the books.

Michele spoke of the history of the parish and our convent. "You'll love Syracuse," Michele said. I followed her as she glided up the attic stairs. "I hope you won't mind this isolated little apartment." I scanned the room. It had a small bathroom, even a shower, a bed much like the one I had had as a novice, with a thin mattress and wire coils. The room felt good.

"It's the best you have," I said, coveting the privacy of it.

Michele let out a sigh. "I'm glad you feel that way. No one wants it because of the extra flight of stairs. Lazy bunch." She laughed. "Incidentally, Lisa phoned," she said.

"Yes, I've been expecting news about college."

"I know. The administration was unable to come to a consensus. Lisa is still working on it. She said not to give up hope."

"It's agony, this waiting," I said.

Michele regarded me silently for a moment. "Lisa assured me she'll let us know by the end of the week. Listen, we've been sewing new habits; the workshop is in the basement. Why don't you get started? I'll help you. It'll take your mind off the Motherhouse." Michele left, trailing behind her an air of charm and sensitive kindness, social graces she wore well and which allowed her to be more acceptable to the narrow minds in our Order and to the priests and parishioners. Would Dr. Jones have wanted her to be tougher, less compromising? I asked myself as I wondered how he would react to my letter, the last act I had performed for St. Anthony's parish.

When I knelt in the back of the chapel, I was warmed

again by the precious beauty of the gold-sealed tabernacle and the lifelike bronze Stations of the Cross. Though different in style, the message was unchanging, unlike my frail human weakness. I begged for Our Lord's blessings. As I dozed from sheer weariness, my thoughts drifted to Jonathan and I allowed them to remain with him.

I found Michele in the basement cutting up old black wool serge habits to make our new short veils. From here on we were to wear navy blue and tan woolen winter suits with knee-length skirts and light blue and beige cotton summer suits. With these we would wear white cotton blouses, nylon hosiery, and any "sensible" street shoes of our choice. We would continue to wear black veils, but now they would be shoulder length, held in place with thin white bands fitted over the tops of our heads, showing our hair and leaving our necks uncovered. We also would wear brassieres, admitting to the world that we had breasts just like other women.

"Sunday we enter the twentieth century," Michele announced as she modeled one of her suits, pushing back her veil to display a generous amount of thick black hair.

"You're good-looking," I said, remembering the smart attractive nuns at Catholic University. Would I be just as tempted to flaunt myself?

Since my seminars with Sister Juliette, I could hardly endure my traditional habit. It had nothing to do with commitment. I was not trying to escape my nun's life-style. Like Michele, I saw this as a new freedom which would enhance, not lessen my role.

Lisa didn't phone until late Saturday night. "Roseann, I'm so sorry for the delay," Lisa began in a businesslike tone. "The administration failed to come to a consensus."

"My God, no!"

"Roseann, listen. Since I'm in charge of the college program, they left the final decision to me." She laughed lightly. "I trust you'll have a fruitful year at Syracuse. You may attend full-time."

"Thank God," I shouted. "I'll never be able to thank you enough," I said.

"Well, Sister Janice helped me get my graduate degree. I rather understand your position. Bless you."

Michele had stepped quietly into the office, eagerly listening to every detail, which I repeated for good measure. However, I didn't share with her the hurt I felt that a consensus had not been reached.

"You're a resident student now." Michele smiled happily. "As far as I'm concerned, you're the captain of your own ship."

Monday, when I drove into the parking lot of Syracuse University, I had no idea how to go about getting a scholarship. I would have to go on my instinct, something I was learning to rely on in my life.

The campus buildings and landscaping had their own special pomp and concrete circumstance. Students, freshmen particularly, milled around, confused, with registration slips dangling in their hands. I walked through a long corridor to the financial director's office, self-conscious in my smart new suit-habit; I was aware of turning a few heads.

Lawrence Vasser stared at me with unabashed surprise. He gestured toward the chair in front of his desk. "Please. I can't remember the time when a pretty nun graced my humble office." He pushed piles of papers aside on his desk and slouched forward, leaning on his elbows. I laid out my needs for the scholarship evenly, praying that he wouldn't detect my uncertainties.

"It rather surprises me, Sister, that your Order isn't providing funds for your college program."

"We had funds for our junior Sisters, a limited amount."

"I also find it a bit curious you've chosen a non-Catholic education system," he added, not too kindly.

"Secular universities have a lot to offer; perhaps, in some respects, much more," I said, trying to keep calm as I watched him keenly. He had the pale skin and soft un-

defined muscles of a man who spent most of his time in-
doors sitting at an office desk.

"How nice you hold us in such esteem," he said dryly.
"You're the only nun who's ever applied for a full scholarship."

"Do you think that too radical, Mr. Vasser?"

"Of course not." He now smiled slightly, pushing a folder
of papers toward me. "Fill these out. Maintain a B average
and you'll be sailing ahead of the wind."

I stifled the urge to step around his desk and hug him
gratefully. Instead, I assumed a religious demeanor, self-
conscious of my exposed legs. "Thank you for your kindness," I said.

Outside, beside a drooping willow tree, I sat on a stone
bench basking in the sun and the pleasure of my victory. I
imagined the surprise on the faces of Mothers Henry, Edmond, and the other counselors when Lisa reported my
scholarship. I was costing them nothing.

Later, as I waited at the registrar's office, I thought once
more about Jonathan. Where was he working in Syracuse?
Would he try to locate me?

The rough voice of the registrar wakened me. She brushed
back black-tinted hair that hardened the angular look of her
features. "Major?"

"Psychology."

"Minor?"

I thought for a moment and then blurted out, "Business."

"Name on your diploma?"

"Diploma?"

"You intend to graduate," she bristled.

"Yes . . . ah . . . Elizabeth Upton."

Her eyebrows shot up. Why not? We had the option now
of using our baptismal names if we wanted. She puffed on a
cigarette. "Go to Section H. Next?"

Curiously, I wondered about using my name Elizabeth. It
felt good, even safe. I gave it no more thought.

*   *   *

I had been into my college program several months when, unexpectedly, Norma and Margaret came to St. Lucy's Convent for an overnight visit while they were attending a convention in Buffalo. When I went to hug Norma, she backed off protectively, smiled, and offered me her hand instead. Her face was pale and there was a look of weariness in her eyes. Her suit jacket was oddly loose-fitting on her left side.

"Have you been sick?" I asked, my eyes drawn to the flatness of her chest. We walked to the recreation room and Norma sank into the couch.

"I'm doing fine now," she said quietly. "I discovered a lump, small at first, but it kept growing." She wove her fingers nervously. "Dr. Stone took tests, said it was cancer. I had a mastectomy."

My hands turned clammy. I could hardly keep my voice steady. "Did they . . . I mean . . . Jesus . . . did they get it all?"

"Yes, they think so, but I'm also having chemotherapy, an extra precaution, you know."

"Lord, help us," I cried out. Silently, I counted the Sisters who had had cancer; nearly fifteen that I knew of since I had entered the convent. I was frightened.

"Norma," I said. "I want to ask a terribly personal favor. Refuse me, certainly. I'll understand."

She looked at me, perplexed, seemingly surprised that I was taking her revelation so badly. The other Sisters accepted her cancer as something to be suffered for the Spouse of Jesus crucified.

"May I see your scar?"

Norma laughed. "You're the first one to ask. Why?"

"Oh, it's just that, well, my imagination gets the better of me, I'm afraid. I feel it might help. That's all." I was surprised she consented.

She disrobed in my bathroom, then covered her body modestly with a robe. Slowly and very carefully, she moved the left side of her robe. The calmness of her expression astonished me, as if there had never been any hurt, any pain in the total acceptance of her condition. I put my hand to my mouth to repress my panic when I stared at the empty scarred cave.

"Jesus save us," I cried out. "Wasn't there some other way?"

"They said it was the best way for me, the only way," she said, in complete control of her emotions. "I'm fine, really I am. A little weak, but my strength is coming back more every day. At the most, I'm a bit lopsided," she laughed, but I couldn't join her.

"What about a special fitting, so you won't look so different side to side?" I couldn't accept her disfigurement, her detachment, or even her faith that she was perfectly fine. She was so unaware that her future would be less merciful than the faith she clung to so heroically.

"Maybe if I were in the world, I could get a special bra."

"Isn't that where you are now?" I asked, sitting down on my cot to hold my cramping stomach.

"You know what I mean." She laughed. "Roseann, we are religious. Our attitudes . . . well, they must not be vain."

I didn't argue the point. She had provided me with a vision I had dreaded to see and now regretted that I had seen.

As soon as Norma and Margaret left for Buffalo the next morning, I phoned Dr. Greco. Because of the length of the trip, he agreed to see me late Saturday afternoon.

I was draped in the white dressing gown, sweat running down my back, when he entered the examination room.

"I'm glad you've come back," he said evenly, looking tired at the end of a long day. I was his last patient, and his nurse seemed anxious to get on with the examination.

"Do you sleep well?"

"Sometimes."

He warmed the stethoscope in his hands before applying the metal disc to my chest. It seemed like a kind thing to do. "How is your appetite?"

"Fine, never have any problems."

"Do you take any vitamins?"

"No."

"I suggest you start."

He dropped my gown to my waist and looked at my naked breasts, then he began to palpate my right breast. I closed my eyes, trying not to feel his fingers move over my breast, slowly exploring, using the flats of his long fingers in small circles to feel the tissue under the skin. He probed the middle of my chest and moved expertly to my left breast. I held my breath.

"Breathe, please!" he said quietly, not losing touch with the rhythm of his movement, and I tensed at the feeling of tenderness. "I am squeezing each nipple to detect exudation," he explained. "Have you been examining your breast in the manner I showed you?" he asked evenly.

"Yes." But I didn't dare say how rarely.

He lifted my gown to cover my naked breasts. "I wish you had come when I asked you to, Sister."

My heart started pounding violently. What had he found?

"I'll be honest with you. I do detect a very small but obviously tender lump. A biopsy is imperative to determine exactly what it is. I can admit you to the hospital right now for tests."

I pulled myself off the table, shaking so much that I could hardly stand up. "No! No! You can't touch me!"

"Please dress. We'll discuss it in my office." He hurried out the door.

I flung on my clothes in a state of panic. Norma's caved-in breast was hammering itself into my brain.

Dr. Greco stood by his window observing me patiently. "The tests will ease your mind. If it's serious, we'll take care of it immediately—the faster, the better; before it gets out of control. Women do this every day. If it's nothing, your mind will be at peace. Living with this horrible fear is nonsense when we can do something about it." As he spoke, I knew he had spoken these same words to hundreds of women before me—and God knows how many nuns.

I found myself clutching at my jacket, pulling it tighter around my waist, as if the faintest exposure would hurt me.

"I saw what happened to one of our Sisters," I said. "Her breast looks like a leper's, her arm's flesh cut off. It's horrible."

"But it had to be done to stop the spread of a fatal disease."

"There has to be another way. I don't want to be cut up." I backed toward the door, my legs almost giving way. "You know. You know what I have, don't you?"

"Honestly, Sister, I don't. That's why we need the tests."

"I won't submit to this humiliation!"

Dr. Greco slid from behind his desk, his arms outstretched. "Calm yourself, please. You don't have any alternative."

"I do."

"Do you intend to cure yourself then?" he asked hotly. "Do you think you're *that* special?!"

"With the grace of God, yes!" I turned and ran from his office to my car. Heal myself . . . oh God! I was losing my mind, nothing seemed clear.

The drive back to Syracuse was long, years long. I'd say nothing to Michele, not now, I thought as I slid unobtrusively into the chapel, where she knelt praying her Rosary, her warm brown skin reflecting the light of the votive candles.

She whispered, "Everything okay?"

I nodded, bowing my head so she wouldn't see my face, my bloodshot eyes. She left me alone in chapel.

I walked to the tabernacle, bargaining with Jesus. "I have given you my best. I have borne my crosses. I don't deserve this. I don't need more lessons." I was afraid to allow my mind to think. I was afraid of myself, of the terror I felt inside me, afraid that I was losing control and attempting things beyond my understanding. I saw Norma's caved-in breast. I wanted to live, not just survive, but this fear was killing me and who could I turn to? Who would understand my craziness?

When I gathered my mail, I still felt like a zombie. For a few moments I stared blankly at a letter from Dr. Ortiz.

Dear Roseann,

It seems my work in the jungle clinics has afforded me a Schweitzerlike notoriety. I've been invited to address the American Psychiatrists' Convention in Syracuse. It would give me great pleasure to see you again . . .

He gave the name of his hotel. "Arrive in four days."

The Sacred Heart had heard my prayer. Dr. Ortiz would listen to me. He might even have answers for me.

"Looking for me?"

I turned to see Dr. Ortiz smiling broadly, his bronze face accentuated by his carefully pressed tropical white linen suit. I felt a rising pleasure at being with him in a hotel dining room, only now premitted because our Holy Rule had changed.

"The wine list will be to your liking, I assure you," he said with a charm I had not before noticed. "They have a formidable array of California reds!"

I smiled at his eagerness. "Why don't you choose for me? Certainly you have more experience in this than I."

He grinned.

I had the good sense to sip my wine slowly; however, even sipping judiciously, I had consumed two glasses by the end of dinner. As we were eating, he talked of his jungle travels and the seminar he would be presenting.

"But why you among so many more conventional psychiatrists?" I asked.

"Maybe they're interested, for a change, in unconventional alternatives. Perhaps they are curious. It's long overdue."

As the waiter brought our check, Dr. Ortiz said, "You've looked so tense all evening, Roseann. We need another place to relax and talk. I suggest we go to my suite." I stiffened in my chair. He anticipated my reaction and calmed me tactfully.

"It has a small delightful garden, a picture-book balcony. It's very serene for a plastic place like this. Come." He rose, beckoning to me, moving my chair. As I slid from the table, he took my hand. The eyes of others in the room followed us. I felt my face flush and I quickly smoothed the wrinkles from my knee-length skirt and adjusted my still unfamiliar short veil.

"Blue becomes you." He laughed, greatly amused.

The suite was as serene as he said it would be. It didn't take long for me to tell him about my medical examination. He had sunk crosslegged onto the heavy carpet, where he sat quietly watching me. His manner was comforting until he spoke.

"You're a violent person, Roseann!"

"I? Violent?"

"I feel you are."

I leaned forward, staring at him. "I don't know what you mean. I'm a nun. My life is dedicated to peace, to love, and to the service of Jesus and His Church."

"Dedicated to love, to peace, all of your nun life?" He sniffed the air. My control was leaving.

"I'll excuse you, Doctor, because you don't understand what's involved in my vowed life. You really have no idea. How can you possibly appreciate its complexity?"

"Keep it up, keep it up. You're putting on a wonderful show, Roseann. You know everything, you have all the answers. I don't know a thing. Egotistical attitude, I'd say."

"It's the truth."

"What do you know about truth, Roseann? You don't know one thing about your body, your breast, your passion, your sexuality, the so-called religious vocation you preach about."

As he hit me with words, I could not think clearly. He had no right to attack me like this. "I do know. I have known," I shouted.

"You claim to know, but you've been hiding behind some ancient myth that this life you live is the *only way* to make it. But it isn't. You've hidden that truth from yourself since you were fifteen."

I held on to the edge of my chair, breathing hard and staring at his blazing eyes. He hadn't moved an inch, though I felt his body sending electric charges all around me.

"I will achieve sainthood!"

"If it kills you!"

"Yes, if it kills me. I will."

"Let it kill you, Roseann. That's what you've been doing for years, letting it kill you. What's this big fuss about the lump on your breast? You've wanted to die for Christ, to become the mutilated St. Agnes, to emulate the agony of St. Joan of Arc! You're the rebel, the interracial do-gooder! Why are you crying on my shoulder? You want to die!"

Sobs were rising in my throat. He watched me calmly. In that moment I hated him, but I couldn't find the words to speak that hate, and he went on.

"My oh my! Pathetic baby! Who are you trying to fool? You'll be exalted. You will be tenderly cared for when your breast is cut out like your Sister Norma's. Your Sisters will tend to you because they'll gain indulgences in heaven. Your grave will lie under that romantic oak tree you've mentioned more than once. You see, Roseann, I haven't forgotten a thing." He glowed like a demon. "You'll get recognition, finally." Every secret I had entrusted to him was slapped back in my face ruthlessly, mocking me.

"Your religious Order will sanctify you, if only for a moment. That's what you want, Roseann. Admit it, for God's sake!"

"Damn you! No! No! I wanted their love." I was on my feet screaming, sobbing.

"What do you care about love?" he said, pointing his finger at me.

"I've given my life for love, love of Christ, love of my religious life, love for the people I've served. My *life* . . ."

"Given your life to death?"

"Yes! Yes! Yes!" I sank to the floor beside him and began pounding my knuckles into the carpet, but it couldn't stop my confusion, my pain, my humiliation.

"Come now, Roseann. You've been living for death, death to self, as they call it in your books. Your body, your soul, have finally agreed to let you get sick, to die. They've had it with you, Roseann. They have begun to take you at your word. It's not at all curious they should attack your left breast, eat at it—the symbol of a woman's love nestled by her heart, nourishment for newborns, for lovers. Interesting indeed!" He spoke now in a clinical tone, seemingly detached from the pain he was inflicting on me.

"I won't let it kill me!" I screamed, digging my fingers into the carpet, as if I were trying to hold on to the earth against the unknown disease sucking the life from me. "I want to live. I want to love. Jesus! I can't stand this." I curled myself into a tight fetal ball, straining for the warm security of the womb, for darkness, for sanctuary—oblivious of where I was or what I was doing.

Then I felt his fingers push me savagely out from my escape hatch, not once but many times, until my ribs burned. "Lift your self-pitying self up, Roseann." I sprang up like a cat, furious at him.

"You can't fight, can you?" he asked.

"I can! I have!" I yelled, trembling. He stood slowly and moved off toward the balcony, breathing deeply of the cool night air.

He turned back to face me. "Fight, then, woman. Fight! Give yourself to passion, to craziness. It cured Jerome eventually. It will heal you as surely as the cowl you gave to him. Do it! Do whatever it takes. You hear me? Do whatever it takes!" By now, I was shaking so that I thought I would fall to the floor again. And though he was fully aware of my physical state, he moved further from me, forcing me to keep my balance. My head began to clear.

"You've created this disease," he said sharply. "Now you must use that same energy to heal yourself. You told Dr. Greco you would do it." I stared at him without blinking, without the fury I had felt, as if my life depended on every word he spoke. "You know what you must do, Roseann, if you want to live. Face your real self, the self you have hidden from all these long years." He smiled gently for the first time.

Unsteadily, I walked toward the door, forcing myself to take control. His voice followed me, "Remove that tarantula's web of guilt that you've been strangling yourself with. You'll be surprised at how your delighted blood cells will respond to the music of your internal freedom. It's enough to heal anyone of any disease." As if to ease the mood and to let me go, he added, "I'll be preaching this to my compadres tomorrow. They'll ridicule my ideas, laugh openly, denounce me as a witch doctor, but in my audience there will be a few who will accept." He searched my face. "And you, my sweet Roseann. Will you have the courage to let go of what is killing you—what is screaming to be released from your breast?"

In that moment I realized he had given me his best. He had pushed me to the edge because I had needed to be shocked; otherwise, nothing would have penetrated my defenses, nothing. He knew this and I felt that he knew more about me than I did about myself. He had given me more caring, more understanding than even I had been willing to give to myself.

I said haltingly, "My dear friend, I promise myself—I promise you—I'm going to get through this, whatever it takes."

He smiled and I walked back to his side. This time I put myself into his arms and kissed him on the cheek. I felt him restraining himself, probably for my sake. He must have known how vulnerable I was at that moment.

Outside the hotel, I sat in the car for a long while, barely conscious of the stream of people moving in and out around me. *Fight for your life . . . you have given yourself to death . . . your body has finally taken you seriously* were shocking truths. He had given me a message I had never heard in the convent or in the Church, and though it seemed radical, there was something inside me that said: Listen. This is a truth you must not discard. I would keep my promises.

I called him the next day to tell him that I was arranging for a three-day private retreat. I needed time and space to deal with what was happening in me. I blessed Michele for the sensitivity in her understanding; she granted my request without questioning my need.

I had made my arrangements and was packing a small bag when the mail came and, with it, a note from Dr. Ortiz:

Dear Roseann,

There were so many things I had wanted to say to you, but then, too much too soon isn't wisdom. However, I want to share with you these thoughts. Do yourself this favor during your retreat. Find for yourself a special moment to love yourself, to love your breasts just as they are. You have created what's in them. Love your entire body, your total self. After you have done this, release the pain, the fear, the lump, whatever you have been imagining it to be. Forget it as if it no longer existed and give yourself up to passion, to your feelings, to your emotions without, I beg of you, any guilt. Trust! Trust in this healing message. You can do it. You've trusted in the unseen God. When the time is right, examine your breast, but only when the time is right. What we believe in, what we love, is the most powerful force in our being. You have abandoned your will to the Church, to the abject denial of your goodness. Now *abandon yourself to the love of God, to your whole-ness, to the guiltlessness of honest self-love.*

I reread Ortiz's letter until I had almost memorized it. I finished my packing and left for the Shrine of the Holy Martyrs.

♼ 23 ♼

As I drove into the Shrine, I was aware of hundreds of trees which seemed to embrace me in their leafy protection. I felt the quiet hush of the sacred ground, where proud Iroquois Indians had massacred Jesuit missionaries long ago. I listened to the awesome quiet and tasted the gentle scented wind drifting down from the hills.

I had found the right place to lose myself in freedom. I was anxious to give myself to it, to ponder Ortiz's marrow-deep counsel, to take stock of my life, of where I was heading in my religious vocation.

I rested on a stone bench and closed my eyes, at first unaware of footsteps approaching on the gravel path. When I opened my eyes, a very old priest was standing in front of me, leaning heavily on a walking stick. "Your first time here, of course."

"Yes, Father," I said.

"You didn't ask how I know," he retorted.

"I suppose you easily see the wonder in the eyes of all first-timers, Father . . . Father . . ."

"Father Edwards."

"I'm Sister Roseann. You said Father Edwards. That reminds me of someone, a Father Edward Barrett."

"Ah." The sigh escaping Edwards's lips seemed to go on forever.

"Do you know him?" I asked.

"Well, knew him, of course. Yes. Wonderful man, brilliant, a bit eccentric he was."

"Did you say *was*."

"He's no longer with us—heart attack, sudden, two weeks ago. I'll be seeing you again," he said, and hobbled off whispering to himself.

Father Barrett dead? I buried my face in my hands, resting them almost on my knees. I told myself that if I kept my head down, I might be able to keep from fainting. My beloved Father Barrett, the fantasy lover-comforter I had carried in my heart and mind all these years. Now I saw the world as if it had a great gaping hole in it, left by his death.

The thought haunted me and I envisioned the hole becoming part of my breast, my breast which I had struck thousands of times when I had said *"Mea culpa!"* Sweet Jesus! I had never realized that I had been striking my left breast, beating myself into submissive repression of guilt and sorrow for all of my "wedded-to-Christ" life—the breast Dr. Ortiz had told me to love, to see as healthy and healed. It was as if the news of Father Barrett's death had lit a beacon of understanding in the dull defensive tunnels of my mind. I understood now what Dr. Ortiz was trying to tell me, how my breast, my body, had finally given in to my demands to give up on joy and happiness and pleasure, and to die. In spite of this revelation, I grieved for Father Barrett in the words of Lamentations: "She weepeth sore in the night, and her tears are on her cheeks . . ." I raised my head. I was surprised my eyes were dry; I thought I had been weeping.

It grew dark and the night life of humming insects grew louder around me. I made my way back to the guest house and stared out the window, watching the North Star. My God! I have been dying for so long, I've had no idea what was happening to me. I bent over and felt my legs, legs that had run long and hard, that had been tan and wind-borne, seasoned to strain and to endurance, legs now soft and weary. I felt the lines in the middle of my forehead, deepen in the attempt to face the dream I had longed for with all the fervor of my young soul—the dream of becoming a saint. I had given up the torch-led Olympics, my twin, my mother, my home. I had refused to look back. Instead, I had dreamed of new worlds to conquer for Christ as His forever-Bride. Yes, there was death here, but I wasn't sure in this moment whether it was me or the dream that was dying. Of what value was my life if the dream was dead? How could I go on and live out my life as a nun without the dream?

I could feel myself digging into the depths of my own soul for understanding. What had I yearned for these many years? To be loved, cherished by my fellow Sisters, to feel their caring, to feel myself, my own heart, my body, even to touch Jesus, other than in faith. Was it never to be? I had been too long empty, starved beyond the Church's renewal. I had loved Father Barrett as a holy man, a priest, and, yes, as a man. I had felt something deep, almost sacred, for Ignacio Ortiz and as much for him as a man. Jonathan! He had never left my memory or my feelings. I could admit it now in this moment. I had felt guilty for these loves.

But not loving is the greatest sin of all, I said almost aloud as I leaned against the window. I drew in the early morning air. It was 3 A.M., and I prayed on my knees. "Lord. My Lord, Creator of the universe, Lord of my soul, I have given myself to You in love. I have hated myself for You in love. Now I will begin to love myself, without guilt, and You will be praised."

Back on my bed, I slept soundly. When I awoke, I felt deeply peaceful for the first time in years. I could almost hear Father Barrett's laughter and feel his presence when I walked, later, near the Stations of the Cross.

For the remainder of my time at the Shrine, I avoided the spacious chapel. Instead, I walked through the dense forest foliage, spying on gray-tailed squirrels, unraveling a rainbow of webbed burrs. I listened to the water hiss happily over moss-covered rocks, and I smiled to myself.

I knew that I would leave the Order. By the suddenness and completeness of the decision, I also knew that I had been working on it somewhere below my level of awareness for a long time. I did not know how or when I would go. There were things yet to be done. I wanted to finish my education. I did feel that the Order owed me that. The only thing I was sure of was that the choice to go had been made.

I wondered when and why it had been made. Was it when I realized, as Ignacio Ortiz had suggested, that I made a wrong decision when I entered the convent as a romantic fifteen-year-old, offering a life of sacrifice in exchange for the promise of an eternity of infinite love from a Heavenly Father? Did it happen during the Retreat of the Smiling Faces, when Father Barrett talked of the joy of loving one another, when he kissed my hands? Did it happen when Maurice and Martha made such a terrible mockery of what should have been the joy of loving one another? Was it during my mother's visit, when I realized how sadly disappointed she was in the person I had become in my cold and impersonal religious life? Was it when Judith taught me that my duty to be true to God did not excuse me from the duty to be true to myself? Was it when Jonathan held me and awakened my first real desire to be a woman loved by a man? Was it because of the freedom Juliette promised I would know when I had learned that being a girl-nun was not enough? I could not sort it out yet. It was one of the most important decisions in my life and I didn't know when or how it had happened. Perhaps it was enough to know that dedication to service and to God need not end even though I would not be a nun for all the days of my life.

I followed the brook deep into the woods, away from the paths where people walked and meditated. I was alone. I slipped out of my clothes and stepped into the water, sinking down until it rushed around my waist and I could splash its coolness on my face. I repeated, "I love me—Roseann—Elizabeth. I love my body, my breasts, my desires." I caught tiny frogs in the water, letting them jump from my hand. I laughed loudly and it felt delicious.

Michele greeted me warmly when I returned to St. Lucy's. "Quite a tan you've got for only a few days."
"Maybe it's inside sunshine for a change."
She laughed with me.
In the days that followed, I rarely attended any of my religious exercises, including Holy Mass. I was surprised at how little this neglect troubled me.

♥ 24 ♥

Returning to the Syracuse campus afforded me the distractions I needed and time away from the convent, even though I had little involvement with the Sisters when I was there.

Early the first afternoon, Lawrence Vasser stopped me in a hallway. He slouched casually against the wall and said, "You've been nominated for a summer scholarship if you're interested." He smiled, looking intently at me.

"I am very interested," I said, avoiding his eyes.

"Stop at my office some time this afternoon to fill out the forms. I know that if we spend the proper time together we'll be able to work it out." He winked a broad wink that seemed to come to me from some where in the 1940s, blatant and obvious.

I laughed out loud. "At least you don't hide your intentions, Mr. Vasser, but you could be less obvious."

I hurried toward the library and perched myself in a secluded corner of the second floor. Though I opened my economics textbook, I was unable to concentrate. I was discovering that I was beautiful and intelligent and charming and that my fellow students liked me; that I was likable for myself, not because of the veil I wore or the status of being a nun. I took more care with my clothes and began to wear colors other than blue in my campus dress. I was left only to wonder why I was still wearing my veil.

The *mea culpa*s of my past were gone, and oddly, the tenderness and pinkness of my left breast seemed less noticeable. In spite of drawing away from the religious structure of my convent life and the Church, I found myself closer to Christ and the spirit of my original commitment than I was during so many years of helpless struggle and hopeless searching.

As I wandered about in my new freedom, I discovered the Onondaga Indian Reservation almost within Syracuse itself, and there I took long contemplative walks. There was something profoundly comforting about these grounds, where I walked and reviewed my reasons for becoming a nun, trying to probe inside my shell to discover how I had changed and what had changed me over these last twenty-one years.

I wrote often to Ignacio Ortiz. He was the only friend in whom I felt I could confide. Now that our mail was no longer read by our Superiors, I also wrote to Eileen to tell her that my life as a nun would soon be over.

My beloved twin, with whom I had always had so much unspoken and unwritten communication, was not surprised, nor did she ask any questions except, "Have you written this to Mother, or would you like me to tell her for you?"

One afternoon, as I traced the path along the outer rim of the reservation, deep in birch and aspen trees, I suddenly realized that college was close to an end for me. I would achieve my degree with honors. The Motherhouse would nod its head but not say, "Well done." It would be the tacit nod that indicated "we expected it of you." But even this degree, which had been so important to me, now took its proper place among the priorities in my life.

I had studiously avoided serious examination of my breast. Instead, I had continued to focus on the wellness of my spirit, which was being nourished by my achievements in class and my growing happy awareness of my body. I prayed, how I prayed, that all this was not madness. Through it all, I felt the right moment would come when I would see for myself if real healing had taken place.

Late in July, after a morning at the Indian reservation, I drove back to the convent. I was in the kitchen looking for the tuna fish I had placed in a back corner of the refrigerator. Perched on a high stool in the herb-smelling kitchen, I propped a book on my lap. I had barely crunched a hefty bite of my sandwich when Sister Marcel appeared in the doorway. "There's a call for you," she said.

I picked up the phone to hear Dr. Greco's nurse.

"You have not returned our phone calls," she hissed before putting Dr. Greco on the line.

"It's amazing to me, Sister, that you haven't responded to my letters or phone calls. I should not have to put up with this sort of nonsense," he said.

"I am sorry," I said.

"You're sorry. You're so sorry. That won't settle the question, Sister. You are much too valuable to risk your health, perhaps your life. I'm telling you that what you are doing to yourself is an irresponsible act."

"You are right, Doctor, as you see it, but I want more time to work it out the way I feel is going to help me." There was a long silence before he spoke.

"What about the lump?"

I said nothing, since I hadn't examined it.

"Oh God, woman, you can't do this to yourself unless, of course, you enjoy the pain of not knowing."

"If I tried to explain, you'd think I was crazy, but I feel what I am doing for myself is a part of what you call medicine. It's a positive force of healing." While I spoke, I could feel his fury reaching me through the telephone wires.

"I've been patient, too patient with you. I've listened to your prophetic message, now listen to me. I have a practice that involves responsibility for other lives."

"You must really think I'm crazy, Dr. Greco."

"Yes," he came back angrily. "And more than I'll say on the phone, at my expense."

"I feel I have been making progress."

"Wonderful. Is the redness gone?"

"Yes, it's barely noticeable. My breast doesn't feel tender, but I have not felt it in the way you showed me. I wanted to wait and—"

He broke in impatiently. "That doesn't mean that the lump is reduced, actually. Examine it now and tell me!"

"I can't do it," I said.

"My God, you need help for your mind, Sister."

"Doctor, listen. I promise you that if by the end of the month it isn't better, I'll see you. I mean it."

"Well, that's something. You've never promised me anything. I might just believe you. But I'm telling you, you're abjectly insane to attach yourself to this holistic, self-imaging cult. I say forget it or I can't continue to be responsible for your case."

"Is that a threat?"

"It is not a threat, only the way I feel. You know where my office is." The phone clicked dully.

I was drained from this encounter and I took myself slowly up the stairs to the safety of my bedroom.

I had developed a healing ritual for myself. First I took my thoughts to the Shrine of the Holy Martyrs, then to the Onondaga Reservation, to the rose aura of light that I tried to see enveloping my breast—my whole person—remembering to feel the penetrating oil of gentleness that it seemed to generate, allowing it to encompass me. Finally, I surrendered myself to the feeling of love, wellness, and joy for my breasts and for my entire body. I stayed with that feeling as long as I could, keeping it from my intellect and releasing it through my body. I felt a greater appreciation for the love of Jesus, for the power of healing in this act of love.

All the fears aroused by Dr. Greco disappeared in these moments. My mind calmed its chatter, giving way to peace and a quiet joy. It was a reward that I had earned for myself, here, physically on earth, in my body and now.

Slowly, I unbuttoned my blouse and bared my breast. I passed my fingers and the palm of my hand over it gently. Three weeks had passed since I had last looked at it or touched it. Was it my imagination? Was it self-delusion? The lump was hardly noticeable, the skin not tender, the pinkness gone entirely.

I rebuttoned my blouse. I wouldn't repeat the ritual until I saw Dr. Greco, but I would be faithful to my promise to continue in the spiritual process I had begun. A great drowsiness took over my body and I surrendered myself to the comfort of deep, deep sleep.

Hours later I awoke to a knock on my door. One of the Sisters had come to tell me that I had a phone call in the office.

"Sister Roseann?" The voice was husky, arrogant. Although I had heard it only a few times nearly ten years ago, it was burned in my memory and was as familiar as any voice I knew.

"Yes, Jonathan," I said, dropping into a chair. Quickly, I pushed the door closed with my foot. "How did you get my number?" I asked.

"Joe Lazano gave it to me." He paused. "Joe talked about you all the time, said it was a pity they took you out of that program. I would like to see you." He sounded so sure of himself, I found myself caught up in his boldness.

"Can you meet me at the Student Union coffee shop at Syracuse University at two o'clock?" I asked.

The fact that I hardly hesitated, that I felt no need to talk further on the phone before meeting him, barely surprised me.

Before I had time to question this, Jonathan said, "No problem. Hey, I look the same. Better!" The phone clicked.

I hurried to arrive at the coffee shop first and I waited at a table, outwardly calm but inwardly in turmoil. A young girl with straight black hair and glasses was standing by my table.

"Can we talk?" she asked eagerly. "I have so many questions to ask. Do you love being a nun? You're so pretty, so young and . . ." I looked past her to the door. "Something wrong?" she asked.

"I'm sorry, I can't talk to you now and I don't have the answers you're looking for."

She lowered her head slightly.

Seeing this as a plea for my attention, I grew angry. "Listen, please," I said. "I'm not the nun you want to explore your religious vocation with. Whatever I might tell you will only add to your confusion."

She searched my face. "So, that's it. You're on the way out," she said accusingly.

"That's right," I answered simply. I turned away from her to look out the window, where a parade of students was coming and going along the tree-lined path. I really was deeply sorry, but there was nothing I could say to her. When I turned back to the room, she was gone. I looked out the window again.

It was as if she was replaced by Jonathan, now standing where she had stood beside the table.

"Glad to see me?" he asked.

I laughed at his vanity. "Yes, it's been a long time."

Jonathan's eyes darted around the room at the pretty young women who pranced back and forth. He was aware of them, and many of them seemed equally aware of him with his tanned, muscular good looks and his air of vital masculinity.

"Ah, Roseann, you sure look nice. It's good to see you out of uniform; now you just need to toss off that veil of yours."

I was lost for words, captivated by his confidence, by the manner in which he simply took charge.

"Listen, I have one more stop to make at the foundry and then we have all afternoon for catching up. Let's go."

"Do you presume that I'm going to take off with you just like that?" I said, testing him and testing myself.

He reached over and pressed my arm lightly. "Why not?" He smiled widely and I broke out laughing. I walked with him to his truck.

In the truck, I closed my eyes for a moment. Was this really happening? His phone call, now riding beside him, an afternoon alone with him without fuss or question. I was surprised that my presence with Jonathan now seemed more natural than forbidden. Maybe this was the rebirth of Elizabeth.

Jonathan turned to me. "Are you always so quiet, or are you speechless just being with me?"

"And are you always so sure of yourself?" I asked.

He grinned. "Always. You might be a woman of the cloth, but I am a man of the world."

Maybe he was right. He seemed the sort of man who knew women, where they were coming from, and what they were feeling. Perhaps it was merely a matter of timing that gave a "man of the world" the edge. But at that moment I really didn't care.

He drove into the foundry's parking lot. "I spend a lot of my time here when I work in Syracuse." The inflection of his voice excited me. Once inside the foundry, the heat from the ovens, the husky sweaty men, and the clanking of cables propelled me into another world, a man's world.

Jonathan guided me past blast ovens, shielding me from the heat with his body. He was looking up at the far wall and waving. I glanced upward and saw a bearded young man on a cat-walk, waving back. "That's my partner," Jonathan said. "Here, take my hand." He almost lifted me up the staircase, our voices lost in the noise of the foundry. I held his hand tightly so my heels wouldn't catch in the corrugated steel rungs, and I was aware that in the effort, I had not taken my eyes off Jonathan.

"This won't take long," he said as he led me into an office, where he closed the door, shutting out the noise.

We looked at each other for a moment before he released his grip on my hand. "This is Joe Haines, Roseann. We're working out an extruding problem."

"Nice to meet you . . . uh . . . Miss?"

"Sister Roseann," Jonathan broke in with a sly wink, and he grinned at Haines.

"It's just like you, Jonathan, to try something no one else has." They went on with a discussion of angles and cantilevers, the language of contractors, which I did not understand.

Back in the truck, driving along, we passed a food stand. Jonathan stopped for a six pack of beer and chips. He spread them out on park grass half a mile from the foundry. "You know," he said, "these past years you've never left my mind. Never. When Joe Lazano told me he knew you, I wanted to tear down to that convent of yours and snatch you."

"Why didn't you?"

"Joe only told me the week before you left New Haven. We got to talking one night—drinking, I might add—and he told me all about your program, about his involvement. We compared notes, and my God, I couldn't believe it was you." He studied me while he pried open a beer can. "Here, enjoy."

I shook my head.

"Come on, take a sip. You might just like it."

I sipped from the can, the fizz running down my chin. "You're right. It's not so bad." I glanced around the park. It was deserted. I was alone with Jonathan. I felt no resistance, no guilt. I was where I wanted to be. Softly, Jonathan touched my shoulder. "Do you always wear this veil?"

"Most of the time," I said. I felt the weight of it lift as he slipped it to the grass.

Without the need for words, Jonathan knew I was ready for him. When he touched my lips with his, it was exactly what I wanted to feel. We kissed once, twice, many more times.

Later, he dropped me off on the campus. "See you tomorrow, same time, same station."

I laughed. "Same time, same station."

In the weeks that followed, we met on and off the campus whenever we could find the time, and the time was always too short before Jonathan would have to leave for work or I for the convent or classes. The progress of our relationship seemed natural, but not the veil, not the fact I was still officially a nun. It was a full and happy time during which I did not let myself look too far into the future. I plunged headlong into my studies, attacking economics and psychology with renewed desire to excel. I wrote long and frequent letters to Ignacio Ortiz, telling him all my secrets. His letters to me, not quite as frequent, were filled with caring and encouragement along with talk of his work.

In the back of my mind I knew I had to get hold of myself. I had to be practical. I had to think of returning to California, to the only place I was sure I could find emotional support. I wondered if this was what happened to women who planned their divorces alone, without their husbands knowing.

Jonathan phoned. "Let's get away for the weekend. We can go to Joe Haines's house at Lake George. I have some friends there. You'll have fun." Lately, he had become increasingly dissatisfied with the brief moments we snatched away from work and school to be together.

"Saturday, ten o'clock?" he asked.

"Fine," I said quickly, before I had time to think about it.

Getting away would be easy enough. Michele was visiting her aunt in Harlem for the weekend. The Sisters were at the Motherhouse for a seminar, except Sister Anthony. I took the time to see that all my duties were done and that Sister Anthony would be aware of my leaving. I didn't want simply to disappear. I pulled my overnight bag from deep in the closet and stacked my few leisure clothes at one end of the bed.

As I left the convent, bag in hand, Sister Anthony was

trimming her beloved rose bushes in front of the convent. She glanced quickly at my bag and met my eyes. Then she shook her head ever so slightly.

Moments later, I was at the corner where Jonathan was waiting. As I got into the truck, I began the now familiar ritual of smiling at him and taking off my veil. Putting it deep inside my bag. Jonathan followed my hands with his eyes.

Ritual! It was so hard to avoid the depth of my Catholic blueprint, my nun life, which consecrated every act as sacred and gave dramatic form to the daily tasks of just plain living. I had gone through most of my life without thinking about what was happening to me. But now I found that in the act of taking off my veil there was a delicious feeling of excitement in the taste of forbidden fruit.

Jonathan broke into my mood, brightening it measurably. "I'm glad you decided to come," he said huskily.

"You didn't give me much chance to say no, did you?" I smiled playfully, teasing him, nudging him gently, excited by the touch of his hard, muscled arm.

"Strike while the iron is hot?" I said, laughing. I ran my hand along the edge of his shoulder, pursing my lips as if to kiss him.

His eyes swept over me as he leaned close. "No strike. No irons. But how about covering you in a blanket of kisses?" With that, his lips touched mine fleetingly, sending an electric charge through my body.

Two hours later, he slowed to take a turn hidden by leafy elms and headed up a rutted dirt road to the top of a hill. Joe's cabin turned out to be a wonderfully rambling Cape Cod-style frame house nestled in a grove of trees, five hundred feet from the Lake George shoreline.

Jonathan unloaded the car and I walked through the tall grass, still wet from heavy morning dew. It was an idyllic setting. There was a feeling of wholeness, of safety about the grounds and the house with the lake below. It held a certain inexplicable familiarity that made me feel lighthearted. Jonathan had the bags out of the car and was balancing a carton of wine, French bread, and cheeses. A V-shaped flock of geese interrupted the quiet, honking their way southward in lazy grace.

Jonathan called out. "Happy?"

"This is beautiful. I never expected such beauty." I said. The sun's rays bounced off him, dappling him like a sleek speckled Appaloosa from the surrounding woods.

"It feels like home," I said, turning to follow him toward the house.

He showed me through the house. On the second floor he opened a door. "This room is yours," he said. The room was large and had a bay window overlooking the lake. With its rustic furniture, polished wood floors, windows that gathered the sensuous breezes blown off the lake, it seemed lifted from a picture book. There was fresh white linen on the bed and a huge mirror over an antique dresser. There was a traditional country washbowl and pitcher sitting on the marble-topped credenza off to the side. The walls were covered with pictures of Joe's family, even a few with Jonathan—and one with him with an attractive red-haired woman at his side. I studied it carefully. Maybe this was his ex-wife. I knew he had been married once. I dismissed the thought; it didn't seem important right now.

I changed into a pair of loose-fitting pants, saved from a parish rummage sale, and a bright pink top. And for the first time since I was fifteen, I daubed on a touch of lipstick.

By the time I came down, Jonathan's friends had arrived. The buzz of their chatter filled the early evening air. Jonathan was busy filling wineglasses for his friends, tending hot coals in the barbecue pit. When he saw me come through the door, he called out, "Elizabeth, come meet everyone." It felt good to be introduced as Elizabeth. It was me, and it felt natural.

Later, when everyone was gone and the dishes had been stacked, Jonathan took my hand and led me down to the shoreline, where the water, mauve-tinted in the sunset, lapped at the rocks. We let the cool, fragrant water flicker over our toes and playfully splashed each other. We stood there holding hands and I wondered if all this was only a wonderful dream.

We walked along the water's edge to a secluded little cove on the lake's north shore. I rolled my pants legs up and waded out a few feet into the water. Jonathan watched me. "It's been ages since I've done this," I said, lost in play as I splashed water at him.

He kicked the water, deep rumbling laughter spilling from him as he splashed me back. Then he took off his shirt and tossed it aside, wading out closer to me. "Got you," he shouted, splashing me again as I threw water wildly in the air, shrieking with laughter and stumbling into the lake up to my waist.

I was laughing so hard I could barely stand when Jonathan dove for me, catching me in his arms. He began to unzip my top and slipped off both my pants and his. He was naked, his body sparkling in the water. My body was ivory white against his tan and I delighted in the contrast.

"Follow me." He pushed into deeper water like a contented dolphin. I followed. Jonathan ducked under like a diving loon, grabbing my ankles, popping me upside down as if I were a companion bird, sending bubbles of air to the surface of the water.

Holding my breath, I dove under, throwing my arms around his waist. We rolled under the water looking at each other, my hair streaming, Jonathan's face wreathed in a smile. Then we broke to the surface screaming, gulping in great gasps of air.

We stumbled from the water onto the shore, hand in hand. We were on the ground embracing; he was pulling my body against his chest, wrapping me tightly between his long, strong thighs. I felt the thrust of his tongue exploring my mouth hungrily. My lips parted as I allowed his tongue free reign, joining his with mine. I kissed him as fervently as he kissed me.

We moved easily in rhythm on the wet shoreline grass,

my body easing into the curves of his with abandon. "Elizabeth," he said. "Honey. It's been too long." His fingertips brushed my cheeks, barely skimming the surface of my skin, yet sending a charge of current through my body. He smiled, his breath becoming increasingly rapid.

A deep flush spread across his face and chest. I turned my face to him and buried it deep into his shoulder. I held him, clinging, probing my fingers into the full firmness of the muscles of his back. I wanted the exquisiteness of this moment to touch eternity. I felt the flickering dance of his tongue over my mouth, down my neck, lingering over my breasts. He planted tiny kisses around the aureole of my nipples, which began to stand erect. He caressed my body with his hands and his thighs, with his lips and with the bristled hairs of his chest, raising excitement in my body, in my heart. He kissed my breasts, cupping them between his lips, pulling gently, sucking them tenderly. My hands were alive with the touch of his skin as I caressed and kneaded the muscles of his thighs and his hard stomach. I found myself at his hardened groin. His lips were on my navel, between my thighs, tasting my sweetness as I stroked his hardness, caressing it, bringing it closer, closer to my own cleft.

"My love," I said, arching my back high, forming a bridge with my body, my thighs spread like welcoming gates in longing for the moment when he would enter my convent-sealed virginal walls.

I nearly recoiled from the shock of the pain of his entry, then suddenly, gently, givingly, I relaxed, spreading wider, taking him all in, feeling my walls gently give. He breathed hard on my neck as he sought to reach the depth of my very being with his body.

Rocking gently, his moans mixed with mine, our wet bodies immersed in each other's love. The rhythm of his pelvis and the thrust of his buttocks increased in intensity. He moved up and my body rose higher, meeting his, wanting only to keep the hardness of him close inside me, filling my emptinesses. Jonathan's whole body seemed to coil and then erupt in a gigantic moment of release. In that moment I felt the same release, filling me with joy.

I had left something behind, a part of my hidden secret self. My walls, so long sealed, had yielded. Jonathan had drawn out through those walls the child that I had been— until now. As his body pulsed with mine and mine with his, I knew, in that secret place where one knows without thinking, that I had changed. The girl-child had left and the woman could grow.

For a long time Jonathan stroked my skin, allowing his hands to explore my body. I felt the subsiding pleasure of completion warming me as he kissed me. He rose and held his hand out to me. As we walked, the fading light caught our naked bodies. Jonathan stopped and moved his fingers through my hair. "Jesus, you're lovely," he said. "More than I had ever dreamed."

When I awoke the next morning, more refreshed than I could ever remember, the heavy aroma of frying bacon and fresh-brewed coffee filled the house. I found Jonathan in the kitchen.

"Hot cakes," he called out, his fork poised over the frying pan.

"He cooks, too," I said happily.

"And does a lot of other things." He winked.

"I'm finding that out," I said.

After breakfast, we drove to Lake George village to window-shop. I was delighted that everyone could see how much a part of each other we were as we walked along, holding hands. The sun grew stronger as the day progressed and Jonathan was anxious to get back to the lake.

The lake breeze through the bay windows was cool, as we made love again on the white linen bed in the old-fashioned bedroom. The breeze caressed us as we caressed each other.

The drive back to Syracuse was over too quickly. We hadn't felt the need to talk.

Two blocks from the convent, he stopped the truck and

held me. "I'll see you tomorrow."

I didn't want to leave him. "I'll phone you," I said as he kissed me lightly, and I slid out of the truck, quickly putting on the wrinkled veil that had been buried deep in my bag.

❦ 25 ❦

I walked the two blocks slowly. I dreaded returning to the convent because it meant facing the decision of when to leave. I knew the time had come. When I entered there was a quietness I had not been aware of for some time.

"Roseann," Michele called to me from her office. She had returned early from Harlem. She looked less rested and serene than when she had left.

"How was your visit?" I asked.

She ignored my question. "You seem to have gotten a lot of sun over these past days," she said. "Was it fun?"

"How did it go? In New York, I mean," I asked in turn, evading her question.

"I'm never happy about returning to Harlem. But," she said, sighing deeply, "that is my cross to bear. I'm going to the Motherhouse tomorrow. Perhaps you'd like to come along. There are Sisters you haven't seen for a long time. They'll want to hear about your recent achievements."

"My achievements?" I said, startled.

"Of course." She looked surprised. "You're almost a graduate."

As she studied me, I knew I had to tell her what was on my mind. I also needed to speak with Mother Henry, so this trip to the Motherhouse would be well timed. Michele watched me steadily as I struggled to explain how I felt about my religious life, about the changes, about my needs, and about wanting intimate relationships instead of chastity. I explained how I had come to this understanding slowly at first, then more quickly since my experience at Catholic University, particularly since my retreat at the Shrine of the Holy Martyrs. I told her about my breast, about my denial, about its healing, and how I was trying to resolve it all.

She listened very quietly and the way in which she listened told me that she understood, that she was more prepared to listen than to lecture me—at least for now. "I cannot live a lie," I said, "pretending to be what I am not. I have agonized over this. I have doubted myself, submitted my breast in grief and guilt and self-hatred. It must end. I'm sick of it, sick of what it's done to me."

"You can't go on with us, Roseann," she said. "Is that what you are trying to say?"

"Yes. I've been suffocating."

Her voice was sad. "I remember an old man, a gardener in my first convent. He said something once about the Church which I've never forgotten. 'We do need a breeze in the Church, but not so strong that it blows out the candles.'"

"What about *my* candle?"

"Your candle," Michele replied gently. "Your candle and Christ's are one; united, they are the light of the world."

"And alone? Is there light when they are separated?"

"I can't answer that for you, Sister. I have never been alone in Christ." She put out her hand as if to touch me, then pulled it back, turned and walked quietly away.

The sound of evening vespers was announced by the raising of voices in chapel. Its sound carried over the convent walls to mingle with the gentle swaying elms that shaded our garden. I did not join the Sisters but retreated to my room, where I sat at my desk to list the questions I would speak about to Mother Henry.

The ride to the Motherhouse was disquieting; the tension of unspoken thoughts hung heavy in the air. Michele hurried off to join a gathering of Sisters. I walked the grounds, visiting the shrines of St. Joseph and St. Francis, stained and pitted from years of acid fog. I returned to the cemetery to walk the Stations of the Cross. I studied the stone and wood carvings of saintly idols, heroes from my past. It seemed ages since I had lived here as a novice. Everything felt smaller, the perception of an adult who returns to her childhood home, and wonders why she had conceived of it as being so grand.

Mother Edmond approached me in the garden. She still wore the traditional habit, her veil tight against her face and not a strand of hair showing.

"Good morning, Mother," I said, resisting the ungracious urge to tell her I was leaving the Order.

"You've done well in your academic work," she announced, withholding the kiss on the cheek we were now permitted.

I felt disappointed in her somehow and I wiped my eyes as I watched her disappear around the garden wall. I have loved you, Edmond. In my youth and my maturing years, I have always loved you. You have been my unchanging idol.

For a moment I closed my eyes; a rush of memories flooded in. I was sixteen again, wearing a long white veil and black flowing habit, rosary beads swinging at my side. "At last a nun," I had shouted to the treetops as I ran to the novitiate. It had been magic—the magic of being called Sister, the magic of being the Bride of Christ, the magic of ritual and ceremony, of being told heaven was mine by virtue of my commitment. Sweet, sweet magic; even sweet sacrifice.

When I reached the Motherhouse foyer, I found Mother Henry standing by the crucifix, its bronze corpus reflecting the sunlight.

"May I speak with you?" I said, feeling the blood rush to my face, oddly conscious of everything—the sound the floorboards made, even the aroma of cooking chicken from the basement kitchen.

"Is it important, Roseann?" she asked, adjusting her gold-rimmed glasses and locking her hands around her elbows.

"Perhaps I should have made an appointment," I offered, "but I wish to discuss my religious vocation with you. I feel the need of a confessor who can counsel me in my decision to leave." They weren't exactly the words I had wanted to say, and they came out in this blunt and awkward manner, making my position worse.

She edged closer to the hanging cross, unwilling to allow me the relief of sitting by the french window, a comfort she shared with all the other Sisters during conference time. It was at this same window that Mother Edmond had interrogated me for my final vows. Nothing had changed in that tiny corner; not the curtains, the marble table, the stola, or the history.

I wanted to open my heart, to reaffirm my affection for my religious community, to reveal how much it tore me to leave my home and those who have been my family since my budding years. I wanted to express my hopes, my dreams, my fears for my future. But the stiffness of her posture froze that feeling in the pit of my stomach. Mother Henry arched her back and raised her chin.

"I don't recall a likely confessor, Roseann. But if one should suggest himself, I will let you know, of course."

"Of course," I repeated. She was politely saying no, consistent with the reaction to Sisters who dared suggest other alternatives to convent life in their quest for holiness. I should not have expected more.

"However," she added, holding my gaze steadily, "I will take this moment to instruct you regarding your allegiance to selfhood, which may be admirable in a secular world gone mad with permissiveness, but which has no place within the sanctity of these cloistered walls. You have failed, Sister Roseann, failed miserably in fulfilling your sacred vows as the Bride of Christ."

"I've been a loyal daughter of the Church," I said, stunned at her judgment.

"Humble yourself long enough to listen. You were privileged to gain a university degree at great cost to the Order."

"I beg to differ. It was at no cost. I earned those scholarships myself."

She ignored my angry retort as she continued. "You have flourished under the protective wings of Mother Church and of our religious Order. Now you show your gratitude by abandoning us and all your cherished ideals, your vows, your dreams for perfection in this pursuit of selfhood. True self is found in our submission to the will of God. You have been given more than your fair portion, and in gratitude," her voice rose, "you claim to have serious doubts about your vocation. You want to leave."

"Let me explain how it has changed for me," I said, knowing I might as well spare myself this pain.

She used the imperial plural. "We are speaking, Roseann."

"I have given my life to the Church and to the Order for twenty-one years."

"And I for thirty," she fired back. "And still I submit. Still I choose to serve. Still I dedicate my heart to the ideals of Mother Church, to this Order, for the rest of my days. I now doubt if you ever had a serious vocation, Sister! You've insisted on your own rights when the real task was to serve the greater good, above your selfish interest, above your self-centered needs. You have refused to subordinate yourself to the task of bringing the Gospel to the world."

"Mother, please. You claim to know my heart. How can the Gospel be served by restriction, repression, oppression, and denial of personal rights? Religious life isn't the only way—or necessarily the most perfect way—not anymore, if you reflect on the recent teachings of the Church."

"You question too much, Roseann, as you dare question me now. We, as Sisters in Christ, are eager to discipline our base emotions eager to restrain our sinful cravings for the crowned glory of eternal life."

"Nothing is base," I said. "It's a matter of perspective. Who can judge who has more truth, more holiness, who is right? It is not our place to be both judge and jury!"

Mother Henry continued as if she had not heard me. "In seeking yourself, your petty satisfactions, you've failed the Church and your Sisters. You have chosen to divorce yourself from Christ."

"No, Mother," I said evenly. "In finding my true self I am becoming true to the graces rising inside me. I don't care if you don't respect what I say, but it is my honest attempt to live my truth that gives honor to God, who lives in me."

She glanced at the chapel door for an instant. Then our eyes met once more. Her anger had begun to diminish.

"We meet, I feel, for the first time now, Roseann," she said, finally seating herself slowly in a high, hard-backed refectory chair. "I remember when you first came to us, your promise in those days, your zeal to minister to the poor. But we never could have spoken then. You are bright, Roseann, but your ego has deluded you into believing that you are seeking truth. Ah, it's a sad delusion. It is pride you are engaging in and not the search for truth. You have drifted far, yet still you have my prayers and those of your Sisters. I want you to take a leave from St. Lucy's Convent and come to the Motherhouse for a year of retreat before making your final decision. It is the only way of knowing the will of God, of casting from yourself this devil's illusion and the damaging effects of your secular education. Take the time, Roseann."

Her manner again became imperial. "If you leave the bosom of Christ now, Roseann, your life will have been a lie. Are you prepared to live with that knowledge?" she asked with the self-assured authority of God's representative. It was a terrible statement, and I took my time answering her.

"I would despair of my life if I believed that. I respect your wisdom and your dedication, but I am at peace with my decision. My religious life has not been a waste. In my heart, I have not failed. Before God, I have not failed."

I knew that my timing was bad, but I rushed ahead. "I want to speak with you," I said, "of finances, of my practical needs. I don't want to be a burden on my family; it would be unfair."

I handed her a small white envelope with a letter requesting a loan to carry me through my first year out of the convent. In silence, she took the envelope, shoved it into her pocket, and moved off toward the stairs without another word.

Mother Edmond was coming down as Mother Henry was ascending—authority figures from my past and my present. I watched as they bowed stiffly and silently to each other.

Returning to St. Lucy's Convent with Michele was painful. I was too upset from my conference with Mother Henry to share anything with her. Before I went to my room, she handed me the official letter form I would copy when I asked the Bishop for dispensation of my vows.

"Roseann," she said simply, "the process is easy these days, with so many nuns leaving their religious orders. Dispensation takes from two to three weeks." Her face tightened and I took the long envelope out of her hands.

"Thank you," I said quietly, seeking the solace of my room.

Mother Henry's accusations of failure were cruel judgments and I lay on my bed and cried for a long time before I went to my desk and began a long letter, pages long, to Ignacio Ortiz. It eased the sadness I felt, the sense of being so terribly alone.

Finally, I fell into a deep sleep with mysterious dreams that somehow eased the pain. When I awoke, the morning sun was shining through my small attic window. I felt more hopeful. Even before I dressed, I typed out my formal request to the Chancery asking for my dispensation of vows—

ten simple lines to the effect that I no longer had a religious vocation and was unable to continue living my vowed life.

It was a strange realization. The formality of severing twenty-one years of religious service would take fewer than twenty-one days. I was certain neither the Bishop nor his assistants would speak to me or make any effort to convince me I was in error.

I wrote short letters to Eileen and to my mother to let them know that the formal process had begun. As I dropped my handful of letters in a mailbox, I had a sudden sense of relief. The choices were made and there was nothing left to do but wait out the process.

But not all the decisions were made. I was still confused and troubled about my relationship with Jonathan. I knew that I had to learn to understand myself better, to be more honest. I had to understand what I wanted from my future and learn to make my choices without the romantic self-delusions that had determined so many of my past ones. Until I could, I wasn't going to enter into any more commitments.

Jonathan was waiting for me in the Student Union coffee shop. He was clutching an enormous paper bag. "Roast beef sandwiches," he said happily.

I nodded as I tried to formulate the words to tell him about my immediate plans to go home. We drove out to the Indian reservation for our lunch.

He was smiling at me. "You know how much I love you; I want you to live with me." For a moment, I looked away. "Well, will you?"

"We'll talk about it." This was the moment I should have told him everything, but I needed more time.

❦ 26 ❦

I waited each day for the letter from the Bishop dispensing me from my vows and for the letter from Mother Henry granting me a loan. I saw Jonathan every day and gave myself to the happiness of being with him. Each time we parted, he pleaded, "Stay with me, please." I never did. I knew that would only make it harder for us to part when it was time for me to go.

It took the Bishop exactly twenty-one days to discharge me with the dispensation of my vows, the substance of twenty-one years melting away like the wax of a burning candle. I reread the letter. As I had expected, they had not asked me to see them or reconsider. My decision was that of just another nun, among many, leaving, an intrusion into more urgent clerical business. The feeling of having my vows so easily and impersonally dispensed with left me cold. Once more I realized how deeply dependent I had become on ritual.

That evening I was joyously surprised by a phone call from Ignacio Ortiz. The sound of his voice cheered me.

"I've just received your recent letter," he said. "I'm not phoning to give you a witch doctor's lecture." He laughed. "But, my dear friend, you're not a failure. That's a personal judgment, something someone calls another when there is nothing left to say. You've never failed to give yourself to what you loved, to what you believed in. If your Superiors call that weakness, I call it passion for life and for loving." He paused.

"I needed to hear that. I really did. How are you, and where are you?" I asked. He sounded so close.

"You won't believe this, but the Psychiatric Association has asked me to give some training seminars throughout the country, even at old Madison State Hospital, that flea-bag institution. I'll be here in Syracuse for a few days."

"My God, how wonderful. I'm supposed to leave this week. I'm going back home, but I wrote you all that."

"When are you leaving?"

"Friday, noon."

"Then we will have time to see each other. How about tomorrow for dinner? I know of a wonderful place."

"Yes, yes!" This had to be a miracle. The mood of happiness at the prospect of seeing Ignacio Ortiz carried me through to the next morning.

Michele met me in the hall, her eyes dark and clouded. She waved me inside her office and shut the door quietly. I knew Mother Henry's letter had arrived. "It grieves me to give you this letter," she said, "but before you open it, let me tell you that your loan has been refused. I'm terribly sorry; I did my best for you."

I gripped the arms of my chair, hardly able to believe what I was hearing. "Refused? Denied a loan?"

She looked past me. "You'll be given some money in addition to your plane fare. It's what Mother Henry feels is an equitable financial arrangement, provided you sign a statement agreeing that it is."

"Never! I asked for a loan, not a handout."

Michele turned to face me. "Mother feels that what she has given you is your fair portion, in excess of charity."

"I'll call her," I shouted, reaching for the phone.

Michele's dark hand pressed on mine. "Don't! Spare yourself. I know her. She thinks she is doing God's will as it affects you, Roseann. Who are we to question the will of God?"

"I question! I question! It's not the will of God. It's the will of an angry and vengeful woman. I have nothing. Nothing to begin my life with . . ."

"But you came to us with nothing, Roseann. No dowry, no gift to the community, no power of your own. You have been given everything in the eyes of the Order. I don't agree, but what I think doesn't matter. I don't have the power either."

I wept angrily. Michele put her hand gently on my shoulder the delicate warmth of her fingertips trying to soothe the punishing tightness of my muscles. "I can stay with you awhile," she offered kindly as I rose.

"No," I said, holding her hands tightly. "I'm better off by myself. It's about time I learned that, don't you think?"

"None of us is better off alone, Roseann," she said, trying to console me. But they were only empty words.

When I met Ignacio at his hotel that evening, it was like returning to the arms of a dear friend. As I told him of this latest blow, he said, "It's over with, Elizabeth. Let it go. You're leaving soon, so let's enjoy the time we have together."

"You're right. I've been in a state of mourning."

He laughed lightly. "Listen, I think you'll like the restaurant I have chosen."

La Parishioner was a tiny fourteen-table restaurant, exceedingly French. The maître d' smiled as he led us to a table. Couples around us were bowed toward each other in intimate coversation. They might have raised their heads had I been wearing my veil, but the veil was past me now, as were my vows, as was my nunhood.

We were seated in a cozy niche on a comfortable banquette surrounded by flourishing coleus, ferns and geraniums in painted yellow, blue, and red pots. "You have wonderful taste for one who lives in jungles among the wild and primitive," I said, delighted with the decor surrounding us.

"Medicine and jungles are one thing, but as you might suspect, Elizabeth, I'm a man of many tastes."

My pulse quickened. Anything I could have said in that moment would have been superfluous. Instinctively, I reached for the tiny crucifix I wore on a delicate chain around my neck. It did not go without notice.

"Elizabeth, you still wish to be reminded of the pain and death when you're preparing to raise yourself from the dead state of your life?" Slowly, his fingers touched the back of my neck; the chain dropped to the table. I felt as if an invisible weight was lifted from me.

I laughed. "Will letting go always be so hard?"

"If you want it to be," he said.

The waiter brought us wine and bread and Ignacio ordered for us.

"Are you surprised," he finally asked, "that I am with you in this manner?"

"Maybe, but then so much has been happening, it seems less strange."

He studied me, his shoulders brushing the back of the padded banquette. Then he broke into rippling streams of laughter. "Who cares?" He broke off a piece of steaming bread and held it tantalizingly under my nose. "Taste," he insisted. I took it from him, biting deeply.

"Tasting is a wonderful pleasure, Elizabeth. You'll want more and you'll want only the best," he said, grinning. This was a side of Ingacio I had not yet experienced and I found myself taken with his charm. I was warmed and excited.

I sipped my wine and ate and thanked God for the freedom I felt. Casually, I glanced out of the leaded-glass window beside our booth. The slanting sunlight was turning green rolling hills into soft buttery colors. I thought how wonderful it would be if we could leave the restaurant hand in hand and go running through the hills.

"Heavy thoughts?" he asked, interrupting my reverie.

"No, but I'm amazed that all the things I thought I wanted to say to you don't seem important right now."

His eyes searched my face for a long moment. "I want you, Elizabeth. I've loved you for years," he said huskily. "You've known that, haven't you?"

"Yes," I answered, averting my eyes, realizing for the first time that I had known.

"I want you more than Jonathan wanted you as Sister Roseann, even as Elizabeth. Don't look away. Look at me."

"Please, Ignacio."

"Don't be shy," he said softly, turning my chin toward his face. "Don't be afraid. You wanted that veil off years before you were aware of it." It was true. Ignacio had known my heart, my secrets, my mind, long before Jonathan, who knew my body, but not my spirit.

"Stop putting barriers between us," he went on. "We're past that. I have loved you, counseled you, and there is much more I want to give you. But do you want me?"

"Want you? My God, I don't know what I want."

"Elizabeth, I'm not intending to put pressure on you. I only want you to be able to sort out your feelings. There is time, plenty of time as far as I'm concerned."

"Let's go," I said. "I feel like walking." We did hold hands.

"I'll be traveling throughout the country giving seminars. I'll even be in Los Angeles in a couple of months."

I laughed. "I'm glad. I really am. I do know I want to see you, be with you again. I've denied so much in my life."

He held my face in his hands and kissed my lips gently.

From where we walked I could see Mount Tahamo rising from the Indian reservation, now becoming a black silhouette against the sunset sky. I told Ignacio of the hours I had walked there, thinking of his words of counsel and encouragement, making the hard choices that had brought me to this moment. I talked of the eagles that nested on the cliffs of the mountainside. I talked of my fears of leaving the convent

Friday, my fears about facing Jonathan with the honesty I knew he deserved from me.

That night I dreamed sweet dreams of Ignacio, my witch doctor, my friend, my spiritual director. He had listened to my pain, read a hundred letters in which I had poured out all my thoughts and fears. Through it all, he had been my silent waiting lover.

The next morning Jonathan met me at our favorite park. He leaped from his truck, encircled me in his arms, and lifted me high in the air. "You sounded so serious on the phone this morning." Then he eased me down his leg, eagerly kissing me.

"Jonathan," I began.

"It can wait," he answered, urgently kissing me again.

"Listen to me!"

His eyes widened in surprise. "Honey, what's wrong?" He took my hands, and I buried my head on his shoulder.

"I want to be with you, but I can't right now. I mean, living with you is out of the question." My voice was more steady than I felt.

"What are you saying, Elizabeth? I told you—everything has been arranged."

"I've been trying to tell you for days. I can't give you enough of myself . . ."

"You're enough, believe me."

"That's not what I mean. You deserve more than a woman who's still seeking, still trying to find herself. I'm not together. I'm afraid I'll end up hurting you, disappointing you. You really don't know me, Jonathan. I don't even know myself as a woman without a veil. My adjustment won't be easy; it'll take time. How long, I don't know."

"You're talking fears that don't matter to me, honey. They're ghosts, trust me."

Maybe I was crazy to leave him, but it was a risk I had to take. We walked through the park for another hour.

"Promise me you'll return soon. Better still, I'll come to

California to you, meet your family, announce my intentions." He held my gaze, searching my eyes with a fierce
determination I had grown so much to love.

"A step at a time," I said. "It's the only way."

"I am a determined man," he smiled, pulling me into his
arms. "I love you, Elizabeth," he whispered. "True, I might
not understand all your ways, but it doesn't matter."

I was sad, because I knew that it did matter.

We drove back to the convent in silence. When he left me
at the convent door, he said, "Friday it's good-bye to your
convent, but not to me."

I smiled. "You're right. No good-byes."

During the last week I had told each Sister individually
that I was leaving. Their reactions were much the same. Silence. No one asked why, and they avoided me even more
afterward. I was the prodigal son who had been given everything in his father's house and yet would leave for the sinful
pleasures of the world. In their eyes, as in Mother Henry's, I
was spiritually blind, a blighted flower unworthy of nourishment.

There was a knock on my attic door. "Phone for you?"
Sister Anthony said.

"You didn't think I would forget you?" Ignacio chuckled.

"No," I said. "You've been on my mind."

"Well then, you are making progress."

I laughed.

"Listen," he continued. "I want you to perform a ritual
before you leave."

"But I've given up rituals."

"Just one more. I want you to go to where the eagles nest
on the reservation, to the mountain you call Tahamo. It will
ready you for your new journey. Promise me you'll do this
for yourself. Just climb to the west cliff. I was there this
morning. It is beautiful."

"But why? It doesn't make sense."

"Just do it. You've lived on blind faith all your nun life.

Do it. I promise you, there is a message for you in the experience."

In Friday's first dawn light, I rose and pulled my bag from the storage room. I folded my veils for the last time and placed them neatly on my desk.

I took Father Barrett's yellowed notes and tore them up. They had served their purpose. I put Ignacio's letters in a brown folder in the bag. Ignacio said he loved me. Was it only kindness at a time when I needed to be told this from my friend? I laughed out loud. How much a force of habit self-denial had become! Still, I felt more at ease denying his love than in accepting what he had told me from his heart.

I wrote a quick note to Judith, telling her I would phone when she returned from her trip to her family. I hoped she would understand.

When I came to Eileen's red scarf, I kissed it. It was the only thing I had brought from my other life, and now I was taking it back with me again.

Slowly, I pushed my statue of the Virgin Mary to the corner of the desk. I put the cross of my final vows in my trunk with my Bible.

The packing was done quickly. I had little to take. Michele had allowed me the use of the car for my morning visit to Tahamo and the drive to the airport. "Leave it there," she had said. "I'll pick it up." It was her gift of understanding that this was the way I wanted it, and she never questioned my reasons. Standing by her office door, Michele silently watched me leave. None of the other Sisters approached me as I walked down the convent stairs for the last time.

For a brief moment I felt the urge to look back at the convent for the last time. But to look back now would be like turning my head from the new direction reaching out to me. I was finished with looking back, and if there was a vow to take, this was it.

I parked in the guest area of the reservation and headed up the path to the mountain. I tied the red scarf to my wrist at the bottom of the mountain and I left there all my idols, the angels and the saints. Suddenly I felt it was Elizabeth, alone, who must climb the rocky crags. I didn't have to climb to the top; there was a ledge about halfway that seemed right for me.

As I moved up the mountain, I was fed by an energy I used to experience when I had run with my sister. Now it seemed even more intense and I lost all sense of time as I pushed my body up, digging my fingers into the earth. I edged my way to the small rocky ledge overlooking the valley. Tahamo was reflected in the stillness of a crystal lake below. I kicked some rocks aside and lay down, the morning sun covering me with warmth. I closed my eyes and dozed.

There was no sound save the moaning wind. Then I heard a fierce, strident screeching. I sprang to my feet, astonished at the great shadow of an eagle in spiral flight, soaring, gliding, riding the wind in total independence, total abandonment, total majesty, high above the green treetops, swooping down only to spin up again, master of his world. In that moment I became one with the eagle in his unbridled soaring, in his courage, in his power, in the image of his spreading wings. I felt wonderfully exhilarated, on a cleansing flight on my own.

It was time to go. I leaned my body against the rocks, reaching for a tiny shrub, gripping it tightly for support. Just as my fingers strained to grasp it, it tore from its shallow roots, throwing me off balance. I tried to dig my feet into the rocks, into the sandy soil, scraping my hands, terrified that I would fall to the bottom. The rocks seemed more slippery, less friendly, and I desperately sought to hold on to anything that would halt my slide. I became immobile, unable to look up or down. "I can't make it," I cried. "I can't."

Every muscle in my body froze. I cursed Ignacio for telling me to do this. What had it gained me? For this terror, a moment of forgetfulness? I'll kill myself if I risk moving. Thoughts of my death roared inside my head as strongly as the wind whistled past my ears. My right foot had been pressed heavily against a rock, which now gave way from the sheer weight of my body. "No. God! No!" I screamed. In that insane moment I had to defeat my panic or it was the end of me.

"Take one step at a time, Elizabeth," I consoled myself out loud. "Just one step. Easy! Easy."

I inched forward, scraping my legs, drawing blood from painful abrasions, digging my fingernails into the earth, grasping at rocks. I had no idea how long I had been punishing my body on the mountain's flanks, fighting the wind that beat against me, convinced that an ugly demon was intent on ripping me from Tahamo's belly. My lips burned dry and I could taste blood inside my mouth from biting them. I crouched into the mountainside to brace myself and, in that instant, allowed myself to shift the weight of my body slightly to my right. Amazingly, it permitted me to relax.

In relaxing into the rock, easing into the mountain, regardless of the wind, I wasn't out of balance, out of control, as I had been. "Work with it. Fall into it. Become one with it," I found myself whispering as I moved steadily downward, no longer on the rigid, straight path I had been forcing myself to follow—a lifelong force of habit. I moved off to the side now and descending became immeasurably easier. I was enraptured by the purity of the moment.

I came to a point in my descent where I was able to look back and see where I had been and look with assurance to where I was heading. Then I began to laugh, allowing my body to slide, to move with the flow of the mountain. I wasn't afraid that I would lose my balance any longer, or my control. I became one with the living flow, with the rock, the wind, and the eagle. I had reached the base of the mountain.

I dropped to the ground. When I looked up, Ignacio was kneeling in the rocky soil ten feet from me, still and smiling.

"You have been here all the time watching me?"

"I have always been with you wherever you were." He

lifted me to my feet, running his fingers through my hair, kissing my eyes gently. "You have only been surviving, Elizabeth. Now you will live."

I turned my face from Tahamo. I still didn't know the direction of my future. But never again would anything need to be safe or sure for all the days of my life.